Light Technology Publishing

presents

The Sedona GUIDE Book of Channeled Wisdom

Featuring a Select Group of Teachers
and the Channels
Through Whom They Speak:

ALBION ✦ Page Bryant
BEARCLAW ✦ Robert Shapiro
E.C. ✦ Bella Karish
GERMANE ✦ Lyssa Royal
GRANDMOTHERS ✦ Lorraine Darn
JOOPAH ✦ Robert Shapiro
SASHA ✦ Lyssa Royal
VYWAMUS ✦ Janet McClure
ZOOSH ✦ Robert Shapiro
and nameless Teachers ✦ Jananda and Nova 8

and Alsgoud Sprinke

ISBN 0-929385-25-X

Joanna Heikens
Cover Art and Chapter 5 Illustrations

Michael Z. Tyree
All Maps, Section Page Design
and Chapter 17 Illustrations

Photographs of Sedona
Tom Dongo

Published by

800-450-0985
www.lighttechnology.com

PO Box 3540
Flagstaff, AZ 86003

*This book is dedicated to the channeling process —
and to all clear channels of light who, in this or other lifetimes,
prepared themselves to bring other-dimensional guidance,
information and energies to this dimension, so as to facilitate
the process of humanity becoming multidimensional.*

We gratefully acknowledge:

Robert Shapiro, who not only first conceived the idea of this book, but when it was completed and we were searching for the perfect title, gave us Sedona GUIDE Book, with its delicious multiple levels of meaning.

Pat Northrup, for connecting us with Page Bryant and Bella Karish.

Lyssa Royal, for transcribing and preliminary organization of the book material.

Margaret Pinyan, for her skillful and intuitive final editing, organization and rearrangement of the material, including the creation of subtitles and table of contents.

Joanna Heikens, for her outrageously beautiful cover.

Michael Tyree, for his meticulous maps.

Tom Dongo, for his beautiful photographs of Sedona.

And **Janet McClure,** for her commitment to the channeling process — and for the love and patience she exhibited toward all who wanted to talk to Vywamus.

O'Ryin Swanson
Publisher

CONTENTS

Vehicles for Individual, System, Planetary and Universal Growth •
• Healing Centers • Expanding into Larger Being •
• By Request Only • Integrating the Grandmother Archetype •

• Old Coding Activated • Relationship to Earth's Chakra System •
• Energy Gridwork Formed Spirals • Vortexes Allow Release of Pressure •
• Mt. Shasta Energies Compared with Sedona's •
• Electric, Magnetic and EM Properties • Personal Vortex Structures
Entrained • Sedona Vortex/Chakra/Color Correlations •
• Dimensional Portals • Secret Canyon and Andromedans •
• Geometric Shapes to Enhance Different Vortexes •

• Auric Molecules Charged • Stimulation, Transformation and Extra-
galactic Communication • Vortexes in Humans • Other Vortex Areas •
• How a Vortex Affects Humans • Sonic Vibrations Create Change •
• Why Some Don't Feel Vortex Energies • Feeling Ill in a Vortex •
• A Vortex As Consciousness • The Greatest Energy Bombardment •
• Moving Meditations Best • ET Bases • ET Appearances •
• Plants and Animals: Representatives •

Part II. ANCIENT AND FUTURE HISTORY

• An Occupation Lasting 400,000 Years • Extraterrestrial Mining Colony •
• An Ascension Center, Past and Future •
• An Underground Crystal City • A Temple Beautiful •
• ET and Alternate-Reality Technologies •

• A Future Resurrected Civilization • The Cyclic Civilization of Mu •
• Power Struggles of the Past • Destruction of the Earth's Binary Moon •
• The "Victory" of the Occlusions and Our Inheritance from Them •
• The Ancient Underground Sea and Its Pink Dolphins • Montezuma's
Well • The Creators of the Sea and the Garden • Radiation Warfare and
Underground Civilization • The Owls and the Golden Warriors •
• Soul Rescuers • Warriors from the Ninth Dimension •

• A Fault Line Described • The Dolphin Connection • Seismic Activity and Vortexes • Crystal Cities • What to Do When You Feel Our Energy Projections • Calibration—Measuring Your Responses • • Future Submersion? • The Calibration Team Described • • Vortex: An Intersection of Different Time-Space Continuums • • Antimatter and Black Holes • Your Polarized Universe • • Zones of Neutrality • Kachina Energy • Maximizing Your Vortex Experience • Inner Earth Linkages • Government Access • • Vortexes: EM Frequencies One Mile Above and Below the Surface • • A Vortex Outbreath and a Probable Reality • Specific Help from Specific Vortexes • Montezuma's Well • Motivation and Expectation • • Experimenting with the Vortexes • The Grand Planetary Matrix • • Navigating from the Pleiades to Earth • Possible Futures, Possible Pasts and Probable Realities • The Crew Members' Local Connections • • Flight Time from the Pleiades • Traveling in Pairs • • Tonight's Calibrations •

Chapter 13. UFO Encounters in Sedona

• Andromedans and Others from the Farthest Reaches • The Vehicle from Sirius • Parked Above Sedona • Preparations for Earth Cleansing • • Government Testing Hybrid Vehicles • Ultrasounds Associated with Earth's Cleansing Preparations • Chapel-Area Temple in the Rocks • • A Crack in Time at Home • Primary ET Portal • Cloudcraft from Arcturus • Bell Rock Navigational Beam; An Overhead Vehicle • • Waving at the Zeta Ship • The Orange Boomerang •

Chapter 14. Sedona, an Ascension Center

• Serapis Bey Ascension Flame Arrives • Imminent Change for Cathedral Rock • Human Tampering with Earth's Magnetic Field • • ET Intervention to Balance Earth • July 11, 1991 •

Part V. A MORE PHYSICAL/EVOLUTIONARY VIEW

Chapter 15. An Overview of the Geophysical Aspects of Vortexes

• Definition of a Vortex • The Vortexes of the World • Effects of the Sun and the Moon on Vortexes • Astronomical Effects of Vortexes • • Effects of Vortexes on Life Forms • The Sedona Vortex •

Chapter 16. The Nature and History of Vortexes

• Altering Light Projections • Tracing Earth's Origin from Its Vortexes • • Locating One's Natural Home on the Planet •

MAP INDEX

Echoes of the Past

by Mary Lou Keller

Because I arrived in Sedona 34 years ago I am able to relate the story of Sedona's early metaphysical beginnings. When I arrived in March 1957, I felt that this area was my long-lost home, a feeling I have never lost. Nor have I ever had a desire to leave in all those years.

During those years, I have read and listened to books and tapes about the vortexes issued by newcomers who claimed to have discovered them. So perhaps it is time now to tell the true story about their discovery.

We must go back several thousand years to find the first people—the Indians—who knew about the vortex energies in this area and came here for healing and spiritual experiences. Then about 28 years ago a small group who called themselves the Ruby Focus arrived in Sedona from Phoenix, saying they were directed by St. Germaine to start a center here. One day they came to my real estate office (a glassed-in front porch of a large home on Highway 179 where I lived, had my church and carried on my business), where they told me a story about channeled information that described an exact location near a vortex where there would be a four-bedroom home and some acreage. From the description, I knew immediately the place they were looking for. (In those days there were very few homes that large available.) I took them to see the property, and they got all excited, saying they felt it was the place they were directed to.

When we returned to my office, they asked if I had a large, round table where they could channel. I took them into my kitchen and got them settled around the table. I was quietly sneaking out when they called me back and insisted I had to be a part of the channeling. Evangeline and Carmen VanPollen headed this group, Evangeline being the main channel. To my amazement, Evangeline was given an enthusiastic go-ahead by

Evangeline and Carmen VanPollen

St. Germaine, Sananda and others. They commented that day that it was located very close to the strongest vortex in this area, which was between two hills on the way to the airport called Saddleback Rock.

The group had only $1000 for earnest money, but they were instructed to open the transaction with that amount and to agree to $4000 more in 30 days, then go into a 90-day escrow, at which time they would have the balance of the money. I was astounded when the owners of the home accepted the offer. This was the most fantastic test of faith I had ever witnessed, and the next four months proved their faith well-founded as the money came in miraculously right on target. The group came up from Phoenix every few weeks to sit up there in the vortex, insisting that I go along and be a part of it. We were directed to do certain chants and affirmations while sending the energy of the vortex to their future property just below. I have to admit I was more than embarrassed sitting out there on the hill doing the chanting, hoping all the time that no one would see me. It was pretty "far out" in those days for a real estate person to be acting this way. I had already suffered much criticism from the orthodox community for teaching hatha yoga—and now *this*?

The elderly couple who started the group had quite a few happy and successful years with their center before they passed on, Evangeline at the age of 87 and Carmen at 91. The reins were handed to others in the group, who changed the name to Rainbow Focus and are still there doing their work. I am proud to say that I had a part in this wonderful example of faith. This group was given knowledge of the vortexes long before anyone else discovered them, except for the ancient Indians.

Over the years I have observed that few people can live that near a vortex for very long. In the Saddlerock subdivision just below the vortex, a year is about average; there is a lot of real estate activity in that area. I personally lived with a small vortex in my backyard for 17 years—every psychic who came to my place pinpointed the exact location; one even buried a crystal in the center of it; and clairvoyants observed that elves, fairies and devas carefully avoided that spot. I kept quiet about it, though—I wanted no hordes tramping through my quiet hideaway. Thus there are more vortexes than *anyone* knows about in this sacred red rock paradise. And there are a lot of mysteries here yet to be solved.

Mary Lou Keller

Mary Lou Keller is the longest practicing realtor in Sedona, having served as broker for Keller Realty for 33 years. She taught the first hatha yoga classes in Sedona and spent many years hosting lecturers, healers, psychics and other interesting people in the Keller Building on Highway 179 where a lovely new shopping center, Hillside Court, is now located. She also established her own church, the Sedona Church of Light, dedicated to all religions and philosophies, in the hope that it would instill in others a desire to open and stretch their minds beyond narrow orthodox beliefs. She has been interested in paths to higher consciousness for over 50 years. Her new office is located in the Safeway Park Sedona Plaza, 2370 Highway 89A, Suite 3. She can be reached at (602) 282-3586 or her office 282-2125, or by writing P.O. Box 616, Sedona, AZ 86336.

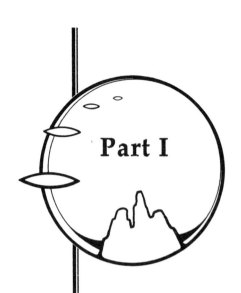

Part I

SEDONA'S UNIQUE
ENERGIES

1

Sacred Sedona
Page Bryant

A special place that was to change my life and perspectives forever was Sedona, Arizona. I visited it for the first time in the mid-seventies between my visits to the pyramids of Egypt, Pele in Hawaii, and the stone circles of Great Britain. Located in the red rock country of north central Arizona in the American Southwest, Sedona is a place of tremendous natural beauty and power. Upon my first visit, I knew this was the place where I wanted to live. My feelings seemed to go much deeper than personal desire, however, for it was also a place that I felt *drawn* to live in, as if there were some purpose for me to be in Sedona that I did not yet realize or understand.

Six years later I moved to Sedona, trusting that I would come to know the reasons why I was certain that being in this place was important and the next step along my spiritual path.

In November 1980 the spiritual teacher I call Albion, for whom I have been the instrument since 1971, channeled to a small group of people information that was to be a turning point in my work. Albion spoke of how over the past century humanity had disconnected itself from nature and from the Earth. As a result, the planet, which was about to enter a time of major geological and climatic changes, must do so in a weakened state. He talked about pollution, toxic wastes, human disregard for the lives in other kingdoms, and many other environmental disasters that we face due to this disconnection. It was time for teachings, given from an esoteric/spiritual perspective, that would, along with the teachings of others, serve to educate the masses about our mistakes and the sufferings on the planet that have resulted from such behavior.

Albion promised to give information and guidance about how we might reconnect ourselves with Mother Earth and change our sense of values about our environment. Albion seemed to have an urgency in his voice that I had not detected before, and I knew that future information to be channeled would be extremely important. The Teacher stated that it was indeed important and necessary for me to live in a place rich in Native American culture and spirituality and possessed of all the geological qualities pertinent to what he had to share. I look back now and realize that the channeling began what has now been a decade of my learning and teaching others what is, in truth, a sacred ecology.

The Living Earth

What first came through Albion concerned the "livingness" of the Earth. I soon came to understand that our planet is a living, evolving organism not unlike ourselves, with purpose, strengths, and weaknesses. The Teacher spoke about the earth's aura (the atmosphere) and her life energy and currents. He told of special places on the earth where the life force of the planet was particularly strong and is coagulated into funnels of energy that he labeled "vortexes," and how these power sites had been recognized by the ancients. The information encouraged me to study the earth and the environment from a scientific perspective, and what I learned, along with the channeling, was put into a book two years later entitled *The Earth Changes Survival Handbook*.

Without doubt the most interesting and practical information that Albion gave is a system of knowledge by and through which we can come to better understand the earth's living force. Without that understanding, Albion knew that we would not see any value in reconnecting ourselves with nature. I have come to call this system of information, designed to help explain the type of life power the Earth possesses, *life energies*. Albion explained that he had need to borrow terms from science to use as definitions of the earth's forces: **electricity, magnetism, and**

electromagnetism. Each of these energies has its own unique power and effect on life forms on the planet. The following is a brief explanation of each life energy, necessary for the reader to understand the system thoroughly.

Electricity

Electricity is the male force in Nature. The planet receives what Albion called "natural" electricity from sources outside herself, including the sun and various solar energies such as cosmic, gamma, x, and radio rays and waves. Likewise, the earth generates electricity, or male "fire" power, from within her own living body. This can be found in lightning; volcanoes; internal heat; hot, dry winds and climate; and mountains. The higher into the earth's atmosphere one travels, the more concentrated is the electricity. Albion also taught that a man-made, and therefore unnatural, source of electricity is cities, due to the high concentration of activity generated by such places.

Electricity affects physical life forms, including humans, in specific ways. Physically, it can elevate the blood pressure and heart rate, increase tension, and can at times manifest as skin rashes, nervousness, and various inflammations and fevers.

Emotionally, electricity amplifies whatever one is experiencing, positive or negative. In intense amounts it can also cause one to be more susceptible to negative outbursts of emotion.

Mentally, natural electricity sharpens the intellect and inspires and motivates the mind, making it easier for one to grasp new ideas and concepts.

Spiritually, the power of electricity can awaken the Soul and the deepest levels of the psyche, as well as activate consciously the intuitive faculties that aid us in our spiritual endeavors and understanding.

Natural electrical locations on the earth include deserts, mountain peaks, and volcanic terrains. Electrical climates are hot and dry. Unnatural electricity is found in cities, war zones, and around power and nuclear plants.

Magnetism

On the other hand, magnetism is the feminine force in nature, and Mother Earth generates her own natural supply. The greatest source of magnetism is water—from oceans, natural springs, rivers, lakes, streams, as well as from rain. Physically, magnetism calms the body and tends to slow down its natural processes. Too much magnetism can cause the body to retain fluid, affect the kidneys and bladder, slow circulation and digestion, cause low blood pressure, and affect the health of the blood.

Emotionally, magnetism in extreme amounts can cause depression, psychological withdrawal, shyness, and difficulty in communicating one's feelings and emotions.

Mentally, magnetism is conducive to psychic ability and experiences, increased intuitiveness, dreams, out-of-body experiences, and other related sensitivities and conditions. It quiets and opens the mind, making it more receptive and perceptive. Magnetism can also give a person easier access to the memory and still deeper recesses of the subconscious, and it increases the flow of creative energy.

Spiritually, natural magnetism helps in directing one along his/her path of inner awareness, which is best reached through meditation, contemplation, and prayer.

Magnetic locations on the earth include most islands and coastal areas, swamps, reefs, and lowlands. A magnetic climate is humid, with many clouds and precipitation in the form of snow, rain, hail, and sleet. The soil in electrical areas tend to be more acidic, whereas in magnetic areas it is more alkaline. Unnatural magnetism can be generated by man-made lakes, dams, and other water-control areas.

Electromagnetism

Natural electromagnetism is a balanced combination of electricity and magnetism. Because it is both male and female in nature, electromagnetism is a powerful, natural healing force generated by the Earth Mother. Through it the planet heals herself and maintains the balance of life force necessary for survival

MARILLA DANTOS

122 Kapodistria str.
Corfu 49100
~~GREECE~~

0030 2661036168
0030 6944183688

email. < marillad@otenet.gr >

You are s

Shamb
Coursing Batch, Glastonbury, Somers
Email:Elisis@talktalk.net

Lost in
Austen.
—
Jemima Rooper
&
Elliot Cowen.
DVD.

Shambhala

Love

With Compliments

Coursing Batch, Glastonbury, Somerset BA68BH UK
Tel: + 44 (0)1458 831797

and growth. Electromagnetism in its most useful form helps to create compatibility and harmony between all life forms on the planet. Likewise, it helps to maintain health and balance within the human body, emotions, mind, and Soul.

Electromagnetic terrain includes waterfalls and wooded areas where there are mountains, such as the Rockies, the Cascades, and the Great Smoky Mountains in North Carolina. The climate generally consists of four full seasons, often with dry and wet periods during the year.

Unnatural electromagnetism results when either the electric or the magnetic content/quality of this balanced energy becomes stronger, totally dominating the other energy. Such would occur if a city were to be built in a natural electromagnetic area, causing the electricity to override the magnetism. This sort of imbalance severely diminishes the natural healing quality of the land.

In humans an electromagnetic imbalance can result in a blockage of the flow of life force. Either the electrical or magnetic could be predominant, resulting from, as a rule, man-made pollution and/or overdevelopment of the land.

After this life-energy system was revealed, Albion suggested that its real value was to provide a classification for natural earth powers. The Teacher instructed us to use the definitions to discover the type of energy wherever we were, as well as the positive and negative effects that we encounter as we live on the Earth. Recognizing these energies and their effects can go far in helping us to reconnect with the Earth Mother and to harmonize with her living powers. Once this is achieved, our sense of values will undoubtedly change, and we can once again live in greater balance and harmony with the earth and all the lives with whom we share the planet.

Vortexes: Part of Earth's Chakra/Etheric-Body System

The next step given in the channeling compared the body of the earth to that of a human, specifically the so-called "etheric" body that mankind possesses, within which are located the chakras and acupuncture points. He said that Earth is no different, and that it too has chakras and acupuncture-type points, or openings in her etheric body through which her life force is emitted in intense amounts. He called these openings vortexes. He explained that these vortexes were known to the ancient peoples worldwide, for our ancestors were then far more connected with the Earth Mother and her natural forces. It was, Albion said, on these vortex sites, some of which are electric, some magnetic, and some electromagnetic, that they built their temples, pyramids, stone circles, medicine wheels, and other sacred structures.

In order to bring the information that he shared with us into a workable symphony of knowledge, the Teacher turned his attention to Sedona. This was, he said, because in the general area of Sedona there is the presence of electrical, magnetic, and electromagnetic types of vortexes. Albion knew this to be unusual because Sedona covers a relatively small area. In fact, it was explained that there are actually seven individual vortexes in Sedona, each with its own charge, fitting it into one of the life energies in his system. One out of the seven was described as a constantly weakening, low-energy, man-made electromagnetic vortex, which has since disappeared completely (Indian Gardens). However, a new vortex has begun to erupt into life, which I will identify later in this chapter.

It was on that chilly November evening in 1980 that the first information regarding the location of the seven Sedona vortexes first came to light. Albion named as the seven energy sites Boynton Canyon; Red Rock Crossing (sometimes known as Baldwin's Crossing); Bell Rock; the Indian Gardens area located a few miles north of Sedona in Oak Creek Canyon; the hill upon which the Sedona post office is situated; a great ledge northwest of Bell Rock that he called Apache Leap; and two red rock knolls located at Airport Mesa.

The Vortexes Categorized; A Negative Vortex Defined

Of these, Bell Rock, Airport Mesa, Apache Leap, and the post office hill were named as electrical vortexes, each having intense charges. One of these, which Albion gave the name Apache Leap, was described as negative in its overall affect. According to him, a negative vortex such as Apache Leap is a site where the natural energies are inverted, drawing energy inward, not unlike a terrestrial black hole. He also stated that this location had been a place where many unfortunate accidents had occurred over time. Albion detailed one such incident involving a group of Apaches who had ridden their horses off the side of this cliff he called Apache Leap rather than be captured by the cavalry. (To this day, I have not been able to verify this as having been an actual historic event.)

The Teacher further implied that there are several negative vortex sites located throughout the world and that they should be avoided. Although they are natural to the body of the earth, they can be dangerous in their effect on human life and consciousness, for they are places where the intensity of planetary power is so great that it has "inverted" on itself, causing a sort of energy collapse. These vortexes can pull a person into them physically, emotionally, and/or mentally, resulting in one's losing control. A few examples given of other negative vortexes were the area of the Persian Gulf, Mount Calvary as the site of the crucifixion, and the so-called Bermuda Triangle. This was an interesting revelation to me personally, as I had done extensive research regarding the phenomena in the Bermuda Triangle in the mid-seventies and had written two books (now out of print) about my experiences there.

A Beacon Vortex

Among the electrical vortexes mentioned, Albion singled out Bell Rock for elaboration, describing it as not only being electrical in charge but a specific kind of vortex that he called a "beacon." Beacon vortexes were identified as sites where energies from outer space enter the aura and, subsequently, the body of Earth, connecting the planet with other celestial bodies within and beyond our solar system. Through these beacon vortexes, located worldwide, the Earth receives and sends energies through what the Teacher described as "celestial ley lines."

Incoming celestial forces empower the planet and assist her in her growth and change. These extraterrestrial powers originate from other planets in the solar system as well as the sun, moon, stars, and galaxies. Through these celestial ley lines

Earth sends her own energy out into space, lending her force to the life of the universe as a whole. Albion explained that the Bell Rock vortex has celestial ley lines that connect it with our moon and the planet Pluto. As the energy from these bodies comes to the Earth, it is transmitted throughout the planetary body by its ley lines. We know from a study of astrology that the moon possesses the feminine force of fertility, growth, and change, whereas Pluto inspires regeneration through purging. These incoming energies not only intensify the natural earth and celestial powers of this special place, but may also be the reason why so many people have had both physical and psychic experiences of extraterrestrial forces and beings at this location.

For years Bell Rock has been associated with UFO sightings. Since the information on the Sedona vortexes was made public in *The Earth Changes Survival Handbook*, Bell Rock has been the site chosen for many special ceremonies by various groups and individuals who believe the magnificent bell-shaped escarpment is a location of Earth-based spaceship operations. Readers will have to determine the validity of such claims on their own (as is true with all information). When Albion gave the information about beacon vortexes, I personally felt that perhaps they facilitate various planetary energies, besides the sun and moon, coming to Earth. This would explain how astrology can describe planetary influences on physical life and consciousness on our planet.

The Teacher also revealed the location of other rare vortexes in various parts of the world. Natural beacon vortexes include Ayers Rock in Australia, Devil's Tower in Wyoming, and the Glastonbury Tor in Somerset, England. Stone Mountain in Georgia and Silbury Hill in Wiltshire, England, were described as even rarer man-made beacons.

Aside from having the usual electrical effects that any natural electric vortex has, Bell Rock is a place where one may access incoming celestial powers, which may be used to elevate the consciousness and sensitize the mind to the most ancient of universal powers and knowledge in the form of archetypes, as described in the works of Dr. Carl Jung and, in more recent times, Joseph Campbell. Many people make pilgrimages to this sacred rock for the purpose of such attunement, and undoubtedly their numbers will increase over time.

Increase in Spiritual Empowerment

Upon visiting an electrical vortex, one is likely to experience an increase in conscious awareness. I suggest that such vortexes are appropriate sites for those who seek greater motivation in their lives and greater personal/spiritual empowerment. Such a vortex also helps individuals become more aware of the Soul, its workings and its impact on their lives and consciousness. I must caution, however, that exposure to too much electricity over long periods of time may result in an experience of negative health and/or negative consciousness. Such a jolt of pure earth power can end in tension, nervousness, or other ill effects. It can be difficult, if not impossible, for some to handle so much power properly. Electrical vortexes should therefore be approached with this clearly in mind.

The same would hold true for those who live in locations that are charged with natural or man-made electricity. Drinking plenty of water, eating a diet with lots of vegetables (which are magnetic foods), wearing the cooler, calmer colors, working consciously with one's creative energy, and taking time daily to relax and release tension are ways to counteract and balance an overabundance of electrical force.

A Time-Warp Vortex

The area around the Sedona post office was also singled out by Albion as an unusual vortex type. This is called a "time warp." Although he said that the one in Sedona is relatively minor in its energy intensity, he wanted to be sure that we clearly understood that these types of sites should not be taken lightly. He described them as anomalies that occur naturally in the atmosphere of the earth and that often have a rather bizarre effect on human perception. Examples of such disturbances were given, suggesting that they can result in time, gravitational, distance, and other perceptual distortions. Examples of other time warps include Gold Hill in Oregon, a place known as "Devil's

Footprints" in North Carolina, and Blowing Rock, North Carolina. He once again included the Bermuda Triangle area, depicting it as a "negative time warp" location.

Boynton Canyon, Native American Sacred Site

The Boynton Canyon vortex was described by the Teacher as the largest of the vortex areas in Sedona; its energy reaches out some twenty-five miles in all directions. However, the epicenter of the vortex, which is in the heart of the canyon itself, is where the power is most intense. The farther out the energy spreads, the weaker its charge becomes. Boynton Canyon is a powerful electromagnetic vortex, giving it healing and balancing strength. I was to discover some months after this information was channeled that this canyon is sacred to the Indians who are indigenous to the Sedona area. The Yavapai Apaches consider it a sort of Garden of Eden, home of the Creator, Spider Grandmother. This explained clearly why Albion had stated in his initial information that Boynton Canyon was "guarded by an Indian elder spirit, a Grandfather whose task it is to protect the sanctity of this most sacred of places." It is a place to go for the purpose of ceremony and/or prayer for healing of body, mind and spirit.

Approximately three years after the initial information was given, Albion informed me that the man-made vortex at Indian Gardens in Oak Creek Canyon had completely disappeared. This vortex, according to what he had stated earlier, was created by a fur trapper who had annually made his way to the southern part of Arizona from the north country, camping and finally settling in the magnificent canyon site. This was an original settlement from which other human settlements grew.

The Birth of a Vortex

The Teacher revealed at the same time that another natural electrical vortex was beginning to open, a powerful geological/spiritual event. Such planetary evolution is not uncommon, however, as can be seen in the gradual birthing of a magnetic vortex into a full-blown ocean in the area we know as the Red Sea in the Middle East. The same thing is occurring at Lake

Baikal in Siberia. Electrical vortexes also occur when new volcanos open up anywhere on the planet.

Albion gave the site of the new Sedona vortex as a point located at the top of Schnebly Hill Road, which he dubbed Sunset Point. He described it as electrical in nature, and over several months he sent two of his students there to offer prayers and do some geomantic work to assist in the birth of the new vortex. This brought the number of Sedona vortexes once again to seven, but all of them are now natural.

Red Rock Crossing, a Unique Sacred Place

The only magnetic vortex in Sedona is located at Red Rock Crossing. Its source of magnetism is Oak Creek. Magnetic vortex sites are excellent places to go if a person desires to relax and tune in to the inner self. Magnetic vortexes help people experience easier access to their memory, extending even into past-life information. They are also good places to go for the purpose of programming one's mind for positive thought and action, prayer, astral travel, and out-of-body experiences, as well as for ceremonies that have to do with cleansing on any and all levels of body and consciousness. In such locations clairvoyance is increased, and one can effectively release tension that has built up over time within the body and mind. Such vortexes also make it much easier to make visual contact with the invisible kingdoms and their inhabitants, such as the angels, nature spirits, and spirit beings.

Albion informed us that the Red Rock Crossing vortex is a site where the presence of two magnificent Archangels stand guard over the "entrance to an inner sanctum," which I took possibly to be a cave where ancient records are kept that record Earth's history over millions of centuries.

Since the channeling of the original information, Albion has continued to elaborate on the Sedona vortexes and other vortexes worldwide, and how we might best use their energies for human growth and evolution. The Teacher has also elaborated on the virtues and uses of electricity, magnetism, and electromagnetism. He has stressed that these life energies are an adequate system that we can tap to link ourselves more firmly with the planet. Within them we may also classify the food that we eat, members of all other kingdoms of life, human personality types, weather conditions and patterns, human behavior and activities, and color, to name a few.

The Energy Grid Systems Embracing Earth

I have recently put all of this information in a book to be released in early 1991, entitled *Terravision: A Traveler's Guide to the Living Planet Earth* (Ballantine Books). The Teacher has also continued to reveal how vortexes worldwide are connected to vortexes of like kind by earth ley lines that interconnect in grids. He described ley lines as geological cords through which natural earth energy flows, distributing the life force throughout the planetary body. Electrical vortexes are linked to other electrical vortexes, magnetic ones to other magnetic ones, and electromagnetic ones to other electromagnetic ones.

Bell Rock, for example (an electrical vortex), is connected to Mt. Shasta in California, the Grand Canyon, Mt. Everest in the Himalayas, and Denali (Mt. McKinley) in Alaska, among others around the globe. Magnetic vortexes such as Red Rock Crossing in Sedona are connected to the island of Bimini in the Bahamas, the Great Barrier Reef, the Florida Everglades, and many others. Furthermore, electromagnetic vortexes like Boynton Canyon are linked to such places as Yellowstone Falls in Wyoming, Niagara Falls in New York, and vortexes in the Smoky, Rocky, Blue Ridge, Appalachian, and Pyrenees mountains. This global grid system in its entirety (according to Albion's teachings) forms the nervous and circulatory systems of the Earth and plays a vital role in maintaining the livingness of the planet.

Since the publication of *The Earth Changes Survival Handbook* (1983) and the release of my initial cassette recording (1982) about the Sedona vortexes, this information has become popularized by aspirants from all over the world. Many teachers and channels have been inspired to come to live and visit the area, and many have offered additional information and comments based on the original material. What is important is that the information serves the purpose for which it was intended by Albion and myself—to help in reconnecting human beings with our Mother, the Earth, so that we might begin to correct some of the severe environmental mistakes we have made, and, hopefully, take a giant step forward in changing our values regarding our planet's fragile ecosystem, of which we are an integral part. Becoming aware of the natural and man-made vortexes worldwide can also help us to identify and place a greater value on the many sacred sites that our ancestors utilized for ceremonial/ spiritual purposes. By making use of this and other related teachings, perhaps we can come to hold Earth in higher esteem and once again truly know her as our Mother.

2

Energies of Sedona
E.C. Through Bella Karish
Channeled 9-17-81

Many present here are not totally aware of or able to totally accept Spirit coming through the human form. But many of you are beginning to realize that when you ask questions of a counselor, a therapist, a leader, or a guide—even when you ask questions and perceive the "still small voice within"— Spirit, that which is your own teachers and guides using Spirit, comes through to give you the answers.

Within the action of all those who have become masters, teachers, guides, and gods to those that believe in them, the Spirit that works through these great ones who have come down to assist you, to help you, and to give you hope has totally been involved with Spirit, which, in this particular case, is the higher beingness of the creative force.

Would that more humans accept that they draw these knowledges to them because you are all Spirit, you're all within the action of speaking from a source beyond your pattern of normalcy. As you well know, there have been many statements to the effect that the human mind has many facets, further areas unknown to man that cannot be tapped until the person is able to accept that there are sources of wisdom other than their minds.

Planet Again Under Attack

We ask you to believe that each of you—especially those that I recognize from my source of Spirit, the heightened awareness present here tonight—are totally involved with great and vast fountains of wisdom, knowledge that must be brought to man because at this time on your planet you are repeating periods of the past in which the planet was under attack. The minds of men, when misused or controlled by powerful agents within these areas, become a source which in turn can defy or defile the mind. The human must accept that within themselves they have something which can turn away or denounce—or, let us say, discourage being controlled in any form whatsoever except by their own spirit and the guidance of those that they trust and know can give them help. Thus this is now a plan in which many of those on earth at this time are returned to be of help to the planet so that Spirit, the gods, the teachers and guides, and the creative force can make your planet once more a place of good, a paradise in the future.

Presently humans are discovering that they are being led to various areas where they are learning a totally different kind of understanding. And many are moving into classes and teachings and developments that in a previous time, even in this lifetime, they have refused to accept.

Ancient Garden of the Giants

At the present time in areas such as Sedona, this channel (within her own memories on the subconscious level, as I give her this knowledge) knows that she has been part of ancient peoples who have lived on this land. Not what you call normal beings, but giants, the Titans of the ancient myths. The gods came down to find a garden, or what is called a paradise area.

Within the energies and the fields of experience here, many of you have been drawn to this particular area because within you is also the same memory. You do not feel like giants, you do not feel like special beings, but you are.

Record Repositories

In an area such as this many different kinds of knowledge were brought and placed into sealed areas in the mountains, much like akashic records that each one has and holds at their past. Within each of the areas here there are those that guard these doorways. They originally were beings. It is the same in places such as Easter Island or areas in Africa or other countries where there are strange massive statues that represent ancient beings. This area is filled with memories of these gods. Within this area there are many different patterns of knowledge held and known, eventually to be read by those who can see into areas of supply. Much of what is here is still not totally understood. Most of those who come here know that their energy becomes heightened and their sensitivity increased. And more and more are gathering to bring about a central force that could in its own way salvage the planet.

A Hub of Balanced Energy

Sedona is a place in which all of the energies are gathered. When and if your earth tilts or shifts, a place such as this will retain its balance like the hub of a wheel, which is the focal point of a force of energy.

Within a heightened awareness of knowledge and understanding of how to do this, humans gather to bring the Light and the force of energy to a certain area that has been such a hub before. Thus each of you who lives here has been drawn here. You know its value and have already begun to sense that you are the center of the planet, in an area that eventually will emanate a force so great that it will balance, harmonize, and fulfill, shall we say, the actions of the future.

Many of you are aware that in your dream state you are involved with strange and unusual experiences. But many do not realize that in their dream state they move about on the subconscious level into areas that they have forgotten, and have forgotten that they have lived in those times and places.

Extraterrestrial Contacts

Some of you receive and have already witnessed the flying wings, the forces of extraterrestrial beings who appear and disappear suddenly and do not make full contact. But they are testing and trying and in every way attempting to reach those that they know accept them and will work with them. For within this area they are all part of the good; nothing that is negative within outer spatial beings.

This means that those who are drawn to Sedona are making a contact on a level that their consciousness is still unable to accept, but will in time. Many of you already know your service and know why you are here. You have been told; you have been shown. Those who do know are a magnet that draws many of those from outside the area to learn, to express, and to be fulfilled for a future that must be better than the past.

Earth Destroyers Gather

Each time a civilization reaches the heights of knowledge, of knowing much about everything that they believe is part of their normal everyday life, it is at this point, within the use or the misuse of that energy, that those who would destroy the planet and all life on it begin to come out of the woodwork. They attempt to overcome, to eliminate the Light of the world and to place themselves in charge, controlling, subduing anything that wishes to be aware. Already you know that there are many on this planet who are involved with gathering groups together to control man.

The Book of Revelations has given you much of this in words and knowledge from Spirit. There are those who realize that there must first be a cleansing of the earth and its particular existence in order to bring about fulfillment of the Plan that says that after these particular forces are overcome, the planet will once more be the paradise of the beginnings.

We ask you to realize that each one has come within this particular area to be part of that Plan to overcome the negative, the evil, and to become part of the Light and the support of a world of such beauty and brilliance that man in his present stage cannot even remember nor will recognize totally as part of the future. Do you have questions?

I understand that someone saw a triangular-shaped object recently in this area.

UFOs

They will see many more different shapes, for each different unidentified object becomes an entry from other existences on other planets or stars, or outside of the periphery of your solar system. Each one is involved with its own particular patterns, or let us call it simply images. These different forms are in the shape or the design that gives certain kinds of energies from their source. Each one uses different methods, not like yours at all, to reach your planet on a level that does not need the same energy fields that you have. Yours on the planet is usually electrical. On other planets or systems it could be electromagnetic fields; it could be a kind of energy you do not know or understand.

Each shape has a different pattern for entry. Inside each of these areas are different kinds of beings also. Some of these who come are of a different form and may simply look down at you, hover over you, seeking to recognize or be recognized, because those who see such objects come from the same source.

Many never see a flying saucer (as you call it) or an unidentified object, although wishing to. This is because the source from which you have come, on the subconscious memory level cannot enter into your field—your field of consciousness as well as your field of energy. Some of the energy on the planet at this time could become detrimental and cause them to dissolve. Therefore they stay outside of your sight or your sensing until they are sure that they recognize those that know them or recognize them from another time and place. Does that answer you?

Yes, it does. Is there some kind of connecting point or an energy capsule, or perhaps even a base or an entry in the Sedona area?

Very definitely. There is a whole field of energy that magnetizes and allows these forms to enter. Again let me point out that the people drawn here who live here are part of the field of energy here, are all part of ancient beings. Not what you call normal human beings but giants, gods, forces of energy from the past that again enter into what is called the center of the earth, the center of the planet, whether you call this the center or not.

There is an energy field here that is a vortex. This vortex becomes a force which draws these energies down. There is going to be contact—in fact, a vast contact between the people here and that which is coming to help, to lift up, if necessary, humans or temporary patterns on the earth as different earth changes come.

Perhaps those earth changes will not come with the violence that they have in the past. You have no memory at the moment in your consciousness of how many times your earth has tilted, moved or shaken, or how the plates of the earth have shattered and moved apart and then back together again. You only know this from certain patterns of science, which knows it only from what they are discovering. Not many know it besides those whose knowledge comes from a different dimension.

Other-Planetary Memories

Many of you have memories of other lives not on this planet but on your own planet or star. You remember your own life force in an area where a system has an earth exactly like yours, with life similar to yours. Many times humans have memories or dreams in which they visit different lands or strange areas. They are experiencing in their memory some other home they have lived in, perhaps even a counterpart of your earth.

It means that in this area there are many compelling forms or forces within the various sectors hidden to the normal world that are attracting from the outer spatial regions that which becomes part of the new age. And which in turn will simply salvage, for the time being, those that need to return to the earth to again rebuild it, restore it as the giants did in the past.

A Communication Center to Other Dimensions

There is much that will occur here within the coming years. And many of those who are now present will live within that particular plan to the point that they will make contact with their own source—here. They could not do this someplace else. They have been drawn here to communicate with their own kingdoms, their own families, their own beingness from another dimension.

Is Sedona the site of an ancient Lemurian city?

Giants/Gods in the Center of Ancient Earth

This area that you are in, as we have said, was a center of the earth in one period in which the gods lived and became totally aware that in time they would have to come outside of the inner earth and begin to rebuild and restore the paradise.

You in this area are part of a perfected civilization that was peopled by gods and giants in the beginning in the center of the earth, which many people feel is molten. It is not.

Each time that the earth turns inside out, or involutes, or the poles twist and turn and change the course of Light upon the planet, that is when the inside turns outside and the outside becomes the inside. Perhaps that is difficult for you to believe. But in many of the areas that are being tested and dug for types of life, are life forms that have come from the inside rather than the surface of the earth. Do you understand?

Do you mean inside or from another area such as the underworld?

There are two kinds of inside world and two kinds of outside world. You know very well that there is such a thing as positive and negative beingness on your planet. There is also evil energy that enters into men and causes them to kill and harm their own brethren. Inside the earth in ancient times when the earth changed, many of these giants—or gods, as you would call them—found that it was time to wait until the outside of the earth was completely cleansed and ready for a new civilization, a new seeding. Some of the gods remained inside the earth, some of them not as positive as others.

This is the constant battle of the positive and the negative energies. Over and over again they come from inside the earth. Many have called them the positive and the negative giants. All of them to a certain point must come out of the inner earth to again be part of the outer earth and to either make up for having been destructive or acknowledge that they have come to be constructive.

The human pattern is a duality. The child that's born is usually involved with two kinds of energies within. The male can be female as much as male. Many people are aware that this is so. Or it could become more female than male, dependent entirely upon the genes in the body and the subconscious memory, as we have told you through the mentor.

The area of knowledge, then, is involved with that which bears a memory of having been part of either positive lifetimes in which good has been done, when the human within his subconscious memory comes to serve others; or a memory of lifetimes of having made errors or causing harm or hurt. One comes back to be of good quality instead of that which is negative.

Within these various energies, then, a human being can go through that which is good and salvaging; and suddenly through some simple action turn into that which is destructive, without being aware of why this occurs.

Emergence of the Giants to Birth on Earth

In these inner earth forms, or beings, have remained and waited for a time in which the earth is to be cleansed or changed, or for civilizations to become part of the new age and new form. They come forward to be involved once more with the acts of the outer beings. However, in coming out, having been inside the earth for so long, they must come through what you call a normal birth path. And so they enter.

Many of you are part of that act, coming forth to be the salvation of the planet, or in some way to be catalysts that change the planet. Whether that is called negative or positive does not matter. It is simply that the giants come forth—entering humans in an attempt to restore, rebalance, reconstruct—or destruct, depending upon the memories involved. Does that answer you?

I'd like to ask about a period of the next seven years, about the people who are in this area now and the people who will be coming to this area. My question is this: What is the highest action, the highest responsibility, the highest type of destiny that those of us can aspire toward and can perform for bringing a greater sense of brotherhood to this area, and influencing the rest of the country and the rest of the world?

Many of you think that this area is like an experiment to repeat an experiment. The magnetic fields here are drawing many who have been here before as part of the "promised land" in a period of time in which it was the only safe place on the planet. This means that the people in your area must realize that they are part of the priest and the priestess patterns of the past.

A Place of Future Safety

Your normal life must go on. But it must be in a way that does not imitate the outside world in a way that becomes overwhelming in a material power or gain. This area has been kept peaceful and clean for many, many centuries. It has become involved with humans that are drawn to it because they realize that it is safety, a place of security in the future.

When the time comes of changes on the earth, perhaps even war, which means a vast form of pollution, the winds in this area, the actions of the cleansing air and wind, can blow away the polluted factors of war. It will occur in a way that those salvaged here will begin a new civilization that will be very much in rightful action.

You are a part of the past and the future, in which those present here become involved with security, salvation, and will give you life and hope.

Prayer and the knowledge that those who come will fit in through this heightened awareness without deteriorating the situation or becoming materialistic or involved with acts that the world is now suffering from—a sickness from the economy's dangers and material power—would be a part of this area in a way that could bring it into being the hope of the world in the future.

I said to you before and I repeat, you could be lifted up by the flying saucers or flying ships, and wait until the earth begins to overcome pollution.

Ancient Knowledge Put to Use

Each one that is drawn here comes not because he knows or thinks he is going to make a living. He comes because in living he makes his life a better one in this area. You will find that many will become involved with ancient knowledges. You will be involved with what you call barter and trade, in which one person—when the time comes and there is little from the outside world that will be brought in—will help another to exist. As in ancient Atlantis when the various areas gathered together, each one produced what was needed for the others.

Money will become something of the past, not just in your area but in your larger area as a part of the economy. The economy already has changed the values and changed the action of humans being able to build or own their own homes as you do here.

It means that you will become a small paradise, a promised land. But you must keep it clean, for up ahead it will be a symbol of the spiritual rather than the material world. Do you understand?

Channeled 9-1-90

There is much here of importance within the pattern of that which is an extremely expressive area of what has been and what will be on planet Earth.

In the beginning, when there were many changes that came about—the tilting, the icing, the flooding of the planet— many of these areas that now seem to be stable were moved and changed in ways that in your particular minds could not be in any way explained except in words of this particular format.

Ancient Polar Tunnels

The pattern of Sedona was the North Pole at one time when the tilting of the earth took place; in another time it was the South Pole. Therefore, tunnels that go from one end of the planet to the other ended in these areas, because it became a central action of use to those who travel from outer space into inner space and then again to the outer regions of the planet— on the outside rather than the inside. The energies that are involved inside the earth are not electrical as on the outside, but magnetic. Thus they are electromagnetic fields that attract like a magnet many of those who are part of these early periods. And one time when the earth was flooded, the entire area of Sedona and its surrounding territory were cities under the sea built to house those who knew and understood there was to be the flooding.

In moving into the earth, similar to that which happened in Atlantis and Lemuria, the pattern became one in which the inner cities had to be built in a way that had air coming from a different source than that which you have in your outside oxygen and the patterns of the outer world. So it became that which, in tubular formats, became a siphoning of the outer atmosphere through these tunnels, energizing into areas that used it, stored it. And it became part of the health and the healing and the life of those who had come into the area to be salvaged from outside attack.

The Temples at the Mountaintops

Sedona is an extremely important area for both space and human existence, for it has everything within it. That means knowledge within the temples that are the tall and great structures now in the area. When it was under the sea, much like that which you know of Pacifica or Hawaii, the action of the tops of these mountains that came into an action of rising and growing (much like you build stalactites and other forms of crystalline format) became the areas of structures that had at the top, like you do in the pyramids, areas in which the space beings could enter, move in, replenish to become humanized so that they could move out when the water receded and be part of repeopling and restoring the earth.

It is a life source, an action which Sedona in its own way is not yet totally able to recover its original power. When the energies of Power and Light come down from space, there come also these dark ones, for they always come where there is Light. Whenever there is an opportunity to rebuild or restore or reconstruct, that which is the ancient power of dark or evil—not just negative, but evil—comes in to be the dark side of the situation. Therefore, within the energy points within various places there are those safe spaces for the Light beings—energy points of great value not only to the humans in the area but to that which remains within the structures inside and outside.

Atlantis Heritage

Atlantis is a symbol of the same situation as Sedona, for in ancient times it was a powerful and great nation within that entire area, a nation of heightened beings who built these towering structures. For they are not made by human hands; they are made by the sources of space in a way that represents the same symbol as the pyramids all over the world (not just in that area, Egypt, other sources of Mexico, etc.).

Pyramids, then, represent the same imagery as that which you find in Sedona, for these structures are built to house within them ancient patterns of knowledge, great libraries of scrolls, much as existed in the time of the oriental beings who came down to the planet from the sun. Thus it is that these actions occur in Sedona.

A Kingdom of the Gods

There was once an action of entering with a wise man into the pattern of the mountains built by the giants to house the prophetic word along with that which was within the earth— the little ones who came in to prepare the earth for those to come. (Within Sedona there were no little ones, for they in no way wished to prepare that area for human life.) It was to be totally a kingdom of the gods, and the gods were to be involved with it only in a way that could manifest and demonstrate their existence within the structures of the giant patterns of mountains and great building forms.

In this action, however, within time and space, there was an evil energy that descended from outer space, not from the surrounding territories. Those from the evil energies found that the gods within this particular territory were doing good, helping, healing the land, and healing those who lived close to the central point of light. Therefore they decided, as they have many times before, that they would send their particular henchmen down into the area to distract in some way those who would listen to their plan to give power to those they called which were not of Light, Love, and Peace.

Dark Energies Move into Water

In various areas where there is a beginning of water fountains or water energy, that which is negative or evil finds an opportunity to move into water, because water has no air within it. It is not necessary for these evil ones to be involved with the air of the atmosphere. They simply need water. Therefore, many times around oceans, around seas and lakes, there is that which is within it that resides and waits for an opportunity to rise up and out into the area of becoming negative/evil rather than good and light. Many times the ancients saw the dragons, the actions of those entities who were involved with strange shape and form—the Hydra and those of the ancient form of the dragon in his evil pattern, breathing fire—actions that were followed by volcanic action. These dragon forms lived in the fire, but always close to lakes or craters filled with water when the volcanic action was completed.

These entrants of the evil chose, as I have said, areas where there was water, but not necessarily running water on the surface. Most of the time it could be on the surface, but much of the time it was underground water and underground wells that could be used for their energy. They needed a different flow, a different kind of situation that could be called oxygen implosion. Within it they could use water in a way that could give them their energy, much as many people move to water to gain energy and balance. So it was with these evil energies, who, using water, slowly but surely began to bring into action their plan to cover the entire area, to submerge again great cities and great land areas.

At this time there is the same implosion within the areas of certain generated actions of the negative/evil energies that wish to submerge the entire territory so that it cannot be a center of Light. They wish it to be covered as it has many times before, without the ability to be used for the good of mankind or the protection of the planet. At this point, then, many coming into the energy of Sedona are part of the ancient tribes, an ancient people who, as in the time of Atlantis, were half men and half gods, or those that you call the Space Beings. Therefore, many in the area who see the spaceships recognize that they are people or sources from their own particular systems.

Some of these humans who are half man and half god have come back into bodies to draw to them either the Light beings or the Dark Beings, because the planet at this point is in dire danger of being submerged by water, by flooding, by a total overlay as in the time of the great flooding of the earth. These events are part of the subconscious memories of some who have been drowned or flooded or overcome because they did not heed the prophetic word to build cities under water and within the mountains that could not in any way be flooded out.

Inside these tall and great structures of red rock there is a complete element of protective shielding—cities that have been built and conceived not through men's building but through that which is the Source of all creation. In these cities are those awaiting the opportunity to once more, when the time is right and the floods recede, come out and rebuild, reconstruct and re-form. However, this is not a plan that at this time is easily understood, for this is desert. How could it become flooded or filled with so much water that the tops of the structures that were islands in the past will become islands again? But always the tops will have an opening for those from other dimensions to enter and become involved with teaching and helping those within who await rebirth, renewal to come out when the floods have gone.

Earthquakes: Uncovering Lost Secrets

The pattern of the cracking open of the earth in certain areas means separation—two sides—over and beyond that which you call recognition of any kind of land, until the waters come as rivers and lakes to fill in the areas of the cracks. There is not much molten energy close to the surface of the planet; it is all in the core, and when it becomes involved with the involution of water from the various actions of flooding, it can cause explosive action in which fire will become steam and steam will become the action of cracking and exploding various areas of the earth.

In Sedona there is protective shielding that may not at this point be totally destroyed if the earth shakes or trembles or moves, but there is a central area that could crack open and reveal certain formats of life and energy within the earth that is waiting to be revealed and brought forward.

There is much here within Sedona that will change when these earth movements begin. But the earth movements will not affect Sedona as much as other areas, for it is a protected area—protected by both inner earth and outer earth. Therefore those who are drawn to it are like those in the past who, reaching safe territory, became helped and healed, not eliminated. But many are also coming to make the same kind of political movement toward material rather than spiritual areas within this territory, to become again like Atlantis with the misuse of energy.

The Assistance of Spacemen

Sedona is a sacred area and may survive if within the future there is a true recognition of the evil energies that have already been noted by some, and if these energies can be and are removed through certain acts by the power of spacemen. It cannot be done by humans, for humans do not recognize that there could be such an evil energy, and therefore would not be able to eliminate this energy except with the help of space. Many are beginning to recognize that the spacemen are arriving to be of help. But there is always that area of space that is part of the negative, which recognizes its own people and will in its own way attempt to join those who are against the ones of the Light.

Within every one of these structures of the high mountainous area is a crystal. A crystal that when gathered together emanates energy and forms a complete pattern of protection that could, would and will keep a shield around this and nearby territory. This will protect the area from man's misuse of power or from a dropping of fire and flame from the sky, much like in Revelations, to devastate various areas on the planet Earth. Sedona could be saved and salvaged by the very fact that it is a space of the Higher Beings who live there within these structures, the tall buildings built by the giants, who only await the time when they can reveal themselves and once more reproduce and reconstruct a new world. Do you have questions?

Each year tens of thousands come to Sedona to visit the vortex areas on a pilgrimage or quest. Are the vortex areas strengthened by this passing crowd or weakened or changed in any marked way?

Use and Misuse of Vortex Energy

Vortexes cannot be changed or weakened, but they can be misused. That means that people who come only for the idea of their own healing, their own ideals, their own ways of wanting to use the energy totally and completely, are misusing this particular pattern of strengthening. It does not lessen the vortexes; it only causes the humans to receive certain energy patterns, and in taking that energy back with them, they become overloaded with the feeling of ego and power, not understanding that it is false power. It is not the true energy. They take it simply to become wealthy, to become rich, to be well, and to be satisfied.

Too many do not recognize that the vortexes are to heighten awareness to bring about a spiritual enlightenment, not simply to change the body structure.

What would be the proper attitude for visitors to have as they visit the vortexes in Sedona?

It is totally impossible to tell humans what to do, for they have become overloaded with the wrong idea of what this energy represents. It is not totally a life energy, nor is it a healing energy. *It is an energy of heightened awareness.* Therefore, they should come solely for the purpose of receiving wisdom and knowledge, with a quiet and a very spiritual approach, simply asking that they be given truths and knowledge. Not asking for health or healing nor money or wealth, but healing for the *spirit*, and lightening and heightening themselves in that respect.

Too many come for curiosity because they have been told these areas have special gifts for them. They are the ones that are sometimes shorted out, as is a person who steps on a live wire. They are not aware that this is similar to a live wire and can either kill or cure. The human is not literally killed, but certain areas within their bodies become shattered by the actions of too much energy poured into their bodies.

The pattern at this point is like a testing ground in which those who come for the use of the good—a heightened awareness and the power of Spirit—find it. Those who come to use it for power to despoil and cause harm not only to the planet but to outside energies, find that also. These, then, are the continuing patterns of good and evil. Sometimes evil succeeds in causing destruction; sometimes the good can overcome it. The act of entering into a power point, an energy placement, occurs because humans (like cars) need a battery charged before the vehicle will work. They go into the area, drawn there by the electromagnetic pull within and outside the earth to bring them power.

A lot of them come to misuse that power. Some of them come to find methods to overcome the misuse of power. It is a battleground much like the ancient Atlantean pattern. It is another Atlantis, except that it is not on the ocean and not in the sea. It is an area that once was covered with water; therefore, those that enter feel the water. They feel the emotional pattern of the water element. It is not there literally but certainly figuratively.

Recently a visitor commented to me (he identified himself as a former CIA agent) that Sedona is now bustling with signs of the invisible government in residence. Some local people are convinced that there are covert government intelligence operations based in this area. Any comment?

Covert Government Activities

Quite right. Let me say that they are, and there are certain covert actions. The point is that here is an area where there is learning and knowledge and wisdom, and those that come from government agencies come to capture and in some way take this particular power and use it in the agencies they belong to. There are certain areas in which there are dark angels who have come to cause a pattern of destruction within the minds of humans.

There are those areas that are using mind control, and those who enter find that only certain areas have the mind-control power. Some of it has already been eliminated, but not all. Mind control is like a hypnotizing pattern in which people receive what they think are answers and knowledge. These humans who enter these areas find that very carefully placed within them are actions that are destructive and discordant rather than balanced and secure.

Are there underground areas in and around Sedona and in canyons that have physical, physical-etheric or etheric beings engaged in some kind of activity, or areas temporarily vacant that are prepared and waiting for such use by any beings?

Shall I point out that we have to some extent pointed out that there is both good and evil in Sedona, each attempting to overcome the other. Either the Light attempts to put out the darkness or the darkness in its own way attempts to put out the Light—a story that is as old as time.

However, that which is darkness hides in the darkness; therefore, there are underground areas in the canyon where the vortexes are not good. They are part of an evil energy rather than good. Humans can walk into them and sense the difference immediately and should not remain in them. For within the area humans have already placed a crystalline substance to block out anything that attempts to reach them.

It does in turn relate to government agencies that wish to use this power—that which is mind control. Actions of overwhelming destructive forces within these territories are vortexes of a different kind. Man must know or feel the difference and not invade that which he cannot handle. Therefore, humans that go seeking or experimenting into an area they have known, but then feel that there is something wrong with the area, should stay away and simply pray that anything that is in it be sealed there so that it cannot move outward and misuse humanity.

It awaits in its particular den, attempting to come out and overcome the Light beings. That battle has gone on in every territory on the planet from the beginning of time. However, the only ones that can truly change, minimize, or lessen it is the source of Light and Power within the Creative Source—the Christed Light. If anyone moves into these areas and feels the attack, he should immediately remove himself from the environment, thus rebuffing any attempts to take him over, for that is the purpose of the evil.

Is there a specific mentor-guardian entity in higher dimensions who is charged with supervising certain destiny objectives for this area (it being understood, of course, that such guidance would not usurp or override individual will)? If so, can this energy field be named or defined so that those of us desiring to can seek alignment with its greater work?

Sedona's Mentor: RA, the Golden One

Yes, of course; RA, the Sun God. That is the One called the Golden One. Let me say that RA has been Ra-Ta and has had many different forms. Aton is part of it; the ancient Adam is part of it. Many different forms have worshiped the sun as the god and the source of all life and energy.

Therefore, the sun is still a part of the very intense involvement with Sedona. It is a land of the sun, not of the sea. Therefore, RA is present in all of his various memories. The sun was the beginning, and the Central Sun was the beginning of all life on your planet. Without the sun there would be death, not life.

What interaction has RA had with this particular area in the past?

He is still present, but not able to do much until there is a change in the action of the area. That will come within the next ten years. There will be a complete change with rivers and water moving through, flooding much of the land in a way that has great and unusual involvement with emotional patterns of the past.

Water is emotion; therefore many humans in the area feel it. As you know, water is the action of oxygen and a mixture of oxygen and air. That is the prime area of the involvement within this territory—water, sun, air. Condensation is very much involved with the territory.

Is it presently indicated that the Sedona area may be impacted by any severe climatic or earth changes within the next ten years?

Earth Changes

As we have stated this, yes, but there will be something that will come about not by nature but man-made acts that will cause situations of desperate and very severe destruction. Not by the good, but by that which wishes to reduce the gods and their use to men.

If they can flood them again as they did in the time of Atlantis, keeping only that which was involved with the evil rather than the good, it could become temporarily overruled with the waters that will flood the area. That would come from the sky as rain beyond man's understanding, much like the floods that caused the people to live on the ship [Noah's ark] that sought to be involved with creature animals and with man.

We know also that the devas play an important part in the well-being of Sedona.

Nature has removed itself to some extent because at this point the devic action does not feel capable of handling situations that are attempting perhaps to cleanse or perhaps to overcome the area. Devic energies are waiting to return, to restore, to renew, and to reconstruct, but first there must be an elimination of the evil before the good can return.

What would you say is the most important information that you can communicate to the readers of this book regarding this material on Sedona, its energies, its ET connections, its purpose, its role in this time of transition and in the years ahead?

A Summary

That is a very broad question, is it not? Let us point out to you that the action of the outer spatial beings is very much involved using the energies of Light and Power within the vortexes of Light, within the structures in which there are many giant gods awaiting the opportunity to come out and help and heal. However, they cannot do anything at this point because there are too many who are not quite aware of the power that is placed within the area of Sedona that could become either extremely vital and useful or that which would devitalize and destroy.

The battle between these energies from outer space and inner space—much like that which has come forth from the various forms of the past who lived inside and were evil, and those who lived inside and were good—at this point await the opportunity to openly declare war against each other. Again, Light attempting to overcome darkness, darkness attempting to overcome Light.

These powers that be are a separate action from that of human beings: therefore the human beings that are drawn to Sedona come because they have been called to be part of this particular pattern of the past, the present, and the future. They come because they belong to these tribal memories of the good and the not-good. They come because they are readying themselves to be part of the battle between good and evil.

At this point we can only say that despite all that has come forth as negative/evil prophecy, there is not going to be a totally destructive pattern on planet Earth. The angelic kingdom will not allow it any more than at the time of Atlantis when all of those who were good found areas of safety within the earth, under the sea—areas in cities built and readied for them.

There are tunnels in the area that extend out to every place within and on the planet, where those who find themselves trapped within an action will find a way out if that is their karmic pattern. Many will be lifted up; we have said this before. That which is evil/negative continues always to try to claim the planet for themselves. Many times the planet has become involved with expressions of destruction on top and inside, to the point that there has to be complete reconstruction over and over again. That is the method by which renewal and rebirth comes about not only to mankind but to the angels and beings of Light who know that no matter what happens, the planet will not be destroyed. The planet *can*not be destroyed. Those areas that have definite placement of the god areas within will manage to salvage and save.

Sedona is a special spot; however, if man does not listen to the Light beings and follows that which speaks of power and control, that can be the difference between Light and darkness.

For those of us who live here year after year in this high-energy spectrum, what is the best easy technique we can use on a daily basis for maintaining optimum balance of life with the energies here?

A Prayer Recommendation

Just to accept that they are Light and Love and Balance. Not necessarily Peace, but Balance. And to ask that all that which is evil, not needed or wanted, be simply returned to its source and sealed there within its own dens, caves, and underground territory—whatever will keep them there so that they cannot harm humanity or the planet. They can do no more than that, to seek it and ask that it may be within the will of the Highest Force.

Man is powerless within the action of good and evil, for within the good many times evil becomes more powerful simply by wishing for power, not Love and Light. It is the same story as from the beginning—the Christ and the Antichrist.

I know there are many people in and around Sedona that are using the mantra/prayer of protection that you've provided through the Fellowship—that what humans do not want is not theirs and in no way do they have to keep it or take it.

If humans recognize that free will is theirs within the creative wish, there will not be loss. There will only be gain in power of Light and fulfillment. Sedona is a special area. It may again become a pole, either a north or south pole, if the planet tilts. If that is so, there will always be others to regain life and begin a whole new action in the future. No one can live forever in the human form, but when the human leaves life, he is reborn into a new life, one of great beauty and fulfillment if he accepts that he has continued life, not left it.

We want to thank you very much for your help and assistance.

Shall we point out that what we bring forth over and over again is sometimes not understood, but in understanding my words they become a fulfillment of purpose. Remember that the Sun God is always that within the Christ energy which remains forever. It does not leave. The Sun is your Life and your Light and that is the s-o-n and s-u-n in its Christed energy. Remember that at all times.

3

Sedona's Unique Global/Cosmic Position

Vywamus Through Janet McClure
Channeled 2/19/90

The Earth has a divine blueprint, a structure. There are those points on the Earth that keep its structure stable, and in some cases help evolve it. Sedona's energy does both. It is a point of stability (although that is difficult to see sometimes), but it is much more a point of dynamic transference or dynamic movement. That is easier to see. Both points are real and are present.

Sedona's Spiritual Guide

There is one great being whose energy guides Sedona and who will soon begin his approach to the Earth. This being is not an individual but an overseer for a group energy. The name is not important, because many will call him different names. The space commands are assisting in facilitating the contact, which, when made with this being, will generate that temple experience I have discussed.

Many of you come to Sedona and don't know why. You are coming in literally on the beam of golden energy that this being is projecting. Because his energy is so strong, it "makes waves" upon Sedona's energy structure—not in a difficult way but in a strong and dynamic and loving way. The association with this being has been getting stronger and stronger ever since the Harmonic Convergence.

Now, this is not just one being but a group of beings with one focus. Their goal is to create in Sedona a temple program that will be fully transformational for those who come and seek within it. Many of you have skills such as healing, and you may be a part of that effort. To reach that point, it is not necessary to set up individual goals but to have individuals and groups come together to coordinate such a large effort. As this great being approaches Sedona, it will become easier and easier to coordinate the effort because his energy is so supportive and so cohesive. Everyone who comes to this point, however, must have let go of most of the ego personality needs that do not create a cohesive effort when the group energy guides the light-stream.

One awakens to the soul guidance, and then the soul leads you to the spiritual focus manifesting upon the Earth, of which you are to be a part. If you have come to Sedona and plan to stay, there is a strong possibility you are to be part of a very large effort that will be made here. How soon? Well, that depends upon humanity and how soon they can bring together their effort without pulling it apart because of group differences. The group interaction is the strength that will make it possible, but only when the personality ego is not part of that which guides the individuals involved.

Vortexes

Vortexes are literally renewal centers for consciousness. They are created rather like a fresh breeze so that consciousness has this renewal capability. It has an energy effect that allows the evolutionary process to be always bringing in a more powerful, and hopefully more balanced, perspective.

Vortexes tend to come together with other vortexes. Thus Sedona's energy points are joining together, and eventually there will be one large vortex. In my opinion there are eight vortexes (although they are not all indicated on maps and so forth) that are presently coming together into one. If you live in Sedona or visit there for awhile, it would benefit you to travel around and be in the center of as many vortexes as you can find. You will find several small ones that are just being born. It may be that you will be the first to experience one of them. If this should be the case, then ask your physical body to help anchor that vortex into the Earth. By working with the Earth's association with this energy, you help yourself and the Earth to become more stable through its use.

In the large developed vortexes, it is important to seek the center for you in that vortex. Bring that energy into your heart and then bring it from your heart into the Earth and allow it to flow back through your physical body. If you do that in each of the major vortexes and then be open to moving around Sedona while carrying ribbons of energy from the vortex, you will literally be helping to weave and integrate *all* of these vortexes into one large one.

A Healing Temple

In my opinion, when this integration has taken place fully (I would say within the next 50-100 years), there will again be a large temple on this site. It will be a healing facility, a very large one for humanity. There will also be a spiritual teacher who helps anchor in that energy. It is now like having ten tops spinning all over. One seeks to bring the ten into one and keep that one balanced so that the whole area becomes more stable. Sedona is not always stabilized in its energy usage, because it is bringing in, not new energy, but a new way to *use* energy that is transformational in the fullest sense. On the frontier of energy usage, it puts you in touch with those parts of yourself that are cosmic in nature and says to you, "Here is the energy to help integrate them."

Depending upon the amount of resistance you have to integrating those parts within yourself, you will have an experience in Sedona that either assists you to make that integration or brings up for you some resistance to look at in regard to it. Probably some of both. While in Sedona you will integrate more into your soul's purpose, and you will also get in touch with certain resistances that then can be resolved. Sedona will bring up for you those areas that need to be looked at because it is processing all aspects of you at the same time. It is bringing them together—awakening the possibilities and helping you to deal with them.

Specific Responses to the Energies

As one utilizes the energies here, first of all they specifically stimulate the level of being called the soul. They seek to allow that level to integrate into the physical structure. Also, they specifically clean out resistances in the spleen and in the energy of the solar plexus.

In a cosmic sense, Sedona is located in the area of the spleen, so it has cosmic correspondences to the physical spleen within each of you. Thus it cleanses and then blends many, many points within a greater perspective. Each cell of the physical structure is united with every other cell in a more complete manner after a trip to Sedona. You could say that the cellular level is literally dunked, or placed into a new level of communication through being in Sedona. If there is a part of you (a Sedona visitor) that you have not understood or have some resistances in, that part will become active in Sedona. A resolution is thus sought that allows full integration within the selves.

Sedona's methodology, then, is one of blending. Through activating each area it thus brings about a more united perspective within self. Cosmically speaking, Sedona's energy is right now [March 1990] being lifted in a manner that ultimately will cause its function not to *become* different but to be *viewed* differently. Its cleansing effect is becoming even more comprehensive, but because of this new level it is helping to lock into the physical structure a connection with what is called the Galactic Core. It does this through an energy-identification process, sorting out vibrationally and linking specifically with the Galactic Core, then drawing it into the physical structure so that this energy may be more easily accepted and assimilated.

A Prime Angelic Site

Sedona becomes an affirmation of the linking with the Galactic Core through the specific energy-linkage system provided by the angelic hosts. Sedona is therefore a prime site of angelic presences, and one easily communicates with other levels of being from there. The space beings flood into the area, especially through this galactic perspective, coming in on specific energy grids identified through an energy resonance. There is a rhythm within Sedona that generates and contributes to waves of consciousness, invoking specific ripples of response from a finer level of being that is galactic and sometimes even universal. This invocation draws and allows those in Sedona to begin to express the integrated point of all of these levels as they experience the Sedona vortexes.

Animal Gatherings

One wonderful thing to watch for in Sedona is the gathering of the animals on the fourth-dimensional, or the etheric level. We may be able to see them; some of them are coming into the dense physical level, too. Use your knowingness when meditating in the energy points, for you may see vast gatherings of animals and birds. They are coming from all over the planet. Not all of them are coming to Sedona, but great groups of them are gathering and uniting, some on the dense physical level and some more on the etheric. There is a lot of change within the animal kingdom that can be seen in this year 1990 and beyond through your energy attunement in Sedona.

4

The Sedona Vortexes: Sound in Motion

Grandmothers Through Lorraine Darr
Channeled 4/2/90

If one were to rise above Sedona to observe the wide-ranging activities in the area, one would perceive a grid point that extends from the core and radiates into the air. This grid point specifically centers both the inflow and outflow of energies in one of the major centers of western United States. It is a threefold action that centers on the part of the grid that is now coming into greater prominence and where many things were centered thousands of years past, now to be awakened to function in this time-space.

Point of Planetary Balance and Individual Reattunement

The other understanding is that Sedona exists in a particular energy field created by the planet over the past 4 million years to be a specific sound emission. It is not that Sedona is famous as "Sedona," but that there are identifiable wave patterns centered here that move in and out of this point in the United States. Sedona is a planetary balance point as well as a point for refining and reattuning human bodies. All who are drawn here participate by bringing their sound, leaving their sound, and allowing their own readjustment and realignment in sound while they are here.

Some vortexes are located on specific lines and in specific spaces created by the lines of the land itself. When a specific function with humans and the planet is completed, the vortex may seem to change or even disappear. The focal point is still there, however, although it has been altered and reprogrammed for the next phase of development of the crust and the deep earth quadrants.

A vortex may have a **spiral** or **laser-beam** form, depending on its function, and each vortex has its own specific qualities. In this area the vortexes are on the surface, although they are beneath the surface in other areas of the United States and on the planet as a whole.

Communication Center

There is also an emanation from this area that maintains communication with the universe. The flows of connections within the solar and the universe systems of which this planet is a part are constantly active, for the planet itself listens and creates and expresses, and these expressions are related to the solar-system constants of Light and the Universal Councils of Administration. The Sedona vortexes are communication centers connecting the local area with the larger United States and planetary grids. They are *dissemination points* for release as well as *freeing points* that accept the incoming flow from the solar system. Thus these energy fields maintain communication both within the planet and points outside it.

Electricity Converted to Sound

From the electrical grid system surrounding the planet vortex energies emanate from deep within the earth and ray into the surface vortex to create an in-and-out movement of sound, or sound in motion, that enables humans to alter their bodies and their understandings. (Humans are often unaware of these sounds, for they exist and function in the octaves above human hearing.) These sounds represent a major reprogramming that will enable humans to begin to perceive, understand, and be fully aware of the grid systems that have existed in the silence, previously invisible. Vortexes are here principally for humans to grow, refine, develop and bloom and for the planet to evolve within the solar system and the solar system within the universe.

Visualize the spiral vortex from within the earth raying out, and from the air raying into the earth (like cones with their open points touching) to aid the planet. Through this open point, or tunnel, pass different "beings" of sound. Each vortex has a different combination of sounds to fulfill its purpose. The human energy field contacts this spiral energy field between one-quarter to three miles from the vortex. The energies can be felt by some people whether they walk into these centers walled off from them or with full acceptance and willingness to become part of the energy. The energy passes nonjudgmentally around the body of those who have walls (sound barriers). The planet knows that humans have walls for their protective needs and that the walls will eventually disappear as the individual's pattern allows.

Human-Vortex Interaction

When people accept the energy, their energy field expands to become the same size as the energy moving in the vortex. This is rather like a sound chamber that automatically responds to what the human requests to be accomplished while there. The vortex responds to this request in a totally objective way, constantly allowing free movement. The vortex accepts the life energies that the individual human gives to it, for this adds to its own structure and power. In essence, the human both contributes and receives, and when this is accomplished the human leaves. There are many who are quite unaware of this process. People are changed by the vortex to the degree of their allowing of their purpose, becoming mobile vortexes that can function with the planet anywhere. It is as if the human becomes an active partner of the planet and the universe.

By agreement within the soul and spirit of the individual, bodies are brought into a vortex of sound at a specific moment for a specific period at an individualized developmental pace. The spiral—or laser beam or silent, weaving threads—in a planetary vortex welcomes the human as it makes an opening sized to the individual's radiated need. In essence, a person comes and participates with a living being—a created form of energy or light—and opens the body to accept the vortex's sound, which is placed throughout that person's spinal column. The vortex feels the various bodies and understands what needs to be accomplished, taking in the singing sound comprised of all of the understandings of that individual. This, in essence, plays the instrument that the human is; and the guiding beings, or guardians, of that individual can then clearly read the pattern of attainment. They can understand where changes are needed and where there needs to be a larger expression (turning on this valve or that valve) on this or that point, accepting that the human becomes aware on more levels of its own vortex patterns. It is like the child coming to the mother/father to be temporarily surrounded and communicated with.

A Cooperative Tuning of the Human Instrument

The guardians (guides) of an individual also grow and expand, and they are aware of what the individual's needs are and what their continuing part is. The radiant actions of the various bodies play and harmonize together, enabling both the vortex and the higher Self to clearly see what has been accomplished through this instrument. Many times the instrument is then attuned another step higher, in turn attuning all body systems to this higher vibration. Then the radiant action from all bodies plays its symphony of sound, and this is given to the air and into the earth for the continued growth in parallel vibrational ways.

The physical body then begins to radiate colors. The other bodies also radiate invisible colors that open and close at a specific vibrational rate. The unity that is thus achieved is not only within the physical body but in the emotional and mental bodies and the body of understandings in all cells. As each body radiates its sound, it accepts a larger purpose, or a greater expression of this sound, which has been activated by the vortex.

Humans can ask to go to school in these vortexes and to be redesigned and realigned. The songs of the humans are accepted into the earth and the air for the healing alteration of the forms of unease that float in the air suspended over the planet, only because humans have forgotten how to take care of these forms of understanding.

Unlocking New Capabilities

The vortex plays its own symphony of sound that readjusts energy centers in all bodies so that they align fully within the physical human body. This realignment allows the physical human body to eventually be known as a craft, a vehicle to be used in many different ways, ways which are gradually unlocked from specific organs and systems of the physical body. This is optional for the human, for it can walk in and be played and walk out again and never be aware of it, though the universe gains by the sound that is released. For the universe knows how to transform sound frequencies for use in different systems to attain specific goals.

Communication through sound comes from the motion of points of light that make up the energy fields, which everything *is* in its aliveness. As you communicate with all of your body and within the physical body, you communicate with the planet, with the body of the solar system, and with the body of the universe. A vortex is the high point at graduation for humans to grow into and become—in its own universe, in its own planet, in its own living, vibrating wavelength of energy. The human is always a part of the overall Plan.

The human quality is important. This is what you term LOVE, spelled with capital letters and radiating like a neon light, yet pulsating when allowed into the physical human body. The waves of sound, a beautiful, knowing understanding can be radiated through a physical body, and can achieve what needs to be achieved in the solar system and in the universes.

The Intelligence of a Vortex

The vortex, as an intelligence, knows what to do, how to do it, how to effect the clearest resonance—and it simply does what is there for it to do. Vortexes are examples for the human race, as humans can learn to be where they need to be, to radiate what they need to radiate, and to receive communication from all systems. Part of their individual purpose is to evolve a clearer expression within the universe and the planetary kingdoms.

It is not as necessary for humans to understand how to use the energies as it is to *become* the energy. A person who allows the energy flow allows *him/herself* to be a useful vortex for personal development and that of earth systems and the planet itself.

A vortex can be like an elevator that goes deep into the knowingness of the planet and high into the knowingness of the invisible parts of all systems and universes. The human can journey into deep caverns of self or into high streams of self on all frequency levels. This is part of the massive transformation humans pass through at specific moments on this planet. Their bodies, souls, and spirit beings can align, can listen to the universe, can polish, cleanse and reform the totality of what humans call consciousness (your energy field) to come into attunement with the visible as well as invisible forms of life.

Humans: Vehicles for Individual, System, Planetary and Universal Growth

For humans are the vehicle for manifestation upon this planet not only for personal and individual growth but for system, planetary, and universal growth as well. All systems function simultaneously. They give the depth and height that is the totality of their being to humans who can walk into the space and temporarily abide in the resonating chamber of the universe to learn. Humans may function for either long or short periods in these spaces in response to the calling of spirit to be manifested within the universal pattern.

To be aware of these activities within the body, the soul and the spirit are to be awakened! Thus a vortex can wake up an individual and start the motor of divine action. Afterward it is up to the individual to continue. This is where humans can learn about allowing the divine (supreme, ultimate, or knowing) action to manifest forms of consciousness that are prepared to function with humans in a kindly yet objective way.

Healing Centers

There is another aspect. When a vortex is used as a healing center (and this is a major function in this area), the centers have already been created; it is the humans who allow themselves to walk into the true center of their consciousness within a vortex. They are forever after a fully operating, functioning, healing center, because healing is only change—the constant flow of the universe. People can consciously obtain healing within a vortex if they, in communicating with that point, agree to allow massive change. Then what you term surgeons, doctors, or transformers are actively called from whatever frequency needs adjustment. They function as one being, a living being of form and structure within the vortex for the time necessary to make the adjustment in the etheric "body of woman" that fills the form-structure of the "body of man." Sometimes instructions are given for several days' rest, sometimes for going to another area of different frequency for a space of hours or days.

Expanding into Larger Being

Each dimension gains by the knowing participation of the human. This participation cleanses and redirects the individual qualities of the mass action of the human wave. It brings the human to a balanced state within its own pattern, and within the pattern of the solar system and the universe. Humans can function within this knowledge and relationship by choice for the remainder of their time on this planet in whatever physical forms they desire to use.

Now, as the human accepts with gratitude and grace to become a larger functioning being, the human has birthed all of man/woman/human into its Being. This is a door opening for humans to learn to use energy flows from all dimensions; and from the wave of the total racial pattern to develop the Whole and the Center Point, which the human is. Humans can walk out of vortexes unlimited and in balance, and they can maintain this. Or they can walk out and be in varying degrees of imbalance, according to their desires, their purpose and their willingness to allow further growth. The act of walking into a vortex comes at specific moments of the individual growth of personality, soul and spirit. These represent growth and transitions on all planes.

The individual can hold imbalance in the personality form and draw more negative energies for the rest of his/her life. Just because someone walks into a vortex does not necessarily denote graduation. There is the continual allowing, participating response from all levels of humans into the totality of the vortex. And the more the human allows this, the more the vortex being permeates the physical human body.

By Request Only

The vortex may not change the imbalance of the individual who walks in unless it is requested, for only the individual can alter the pattern, with the help of the soul and spirit. From that point on, balanced and centered humans can use vortexes to make gigantic leaps in their growth, because every leap radiates new sounds into the planet and the earth for the growth of all. A physical body is an antenna, a receiving/sending station to be developed if one so desires. If you maintain balance, you can make monumental growth and participate in the universal understandings as much as you desire.

Yet to be consciously aware of the overall plan within the joy, the peace and the grace that is accepted and developed in the physical human structure, it is the creative, delighted humans who have the capacities waiting to be used. This is the purpose and full development and attainment of humans becoming hu-man, or radiant, colored beings who will radiate life with a far greater intensity than they thought they could. And who will create and recreate, design and redesign, and fulfill within the body of the universe that which is in the pattern of the solar system to be fulfilled for a particular quadrant or area. This knowing opens when the ability to function in a balanced way is there. The knowingness aids in maintaining the balance and carries along the pattern.

Integrating the Grandmother Archetype

The grandmothers abide in the nature of humans to live again in the human child. Together there shall be creative, delighted humans in their fullness, able to live and function in many ways not only on this planet but throughout the solar system. And this is where we go, walking side by side, parallel and integrated structures of light and form, joyous to know one another again, and to meet soul and spirit in our journeys as they pass through all dimensions and all consciousness and the totality of being.

It has been enjoyable to participate with you and to share your life. We abide in the heart when you allow it. Be your life. Become your lighted being. The vortex is the workshop, the healing center. This area is a healing center. The planet is accepting human life. So be it.

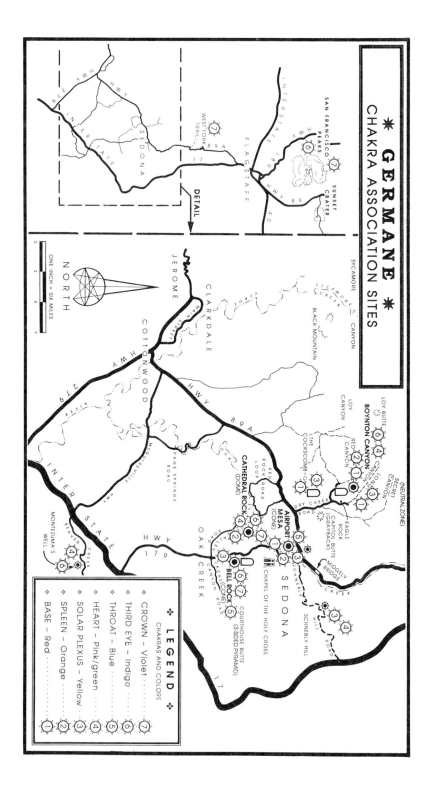

5

Sedona Vortex Questions Answered

Germane Through Lyssa Royal
Channeled 3/1/90

*W*hat is it that makes the Sedona energy so powerful? What
was that imprinting or infusion that created that powerful
energy?

Old Coding Activated

Having many vortexes in Sedona represents to your planet your connections, your very primal connections. *When you
come here and interact with the energy you cannot help but activate
old codes.* When the initial energy imprinted the gridwork of
your planet, at first it was not conscious. Some of the major vortex areas of the planet were not conscious. Sedona was *consciously* imprinted as an area of your planet that is designed not
necessarily for individuals to live in but to pass through. Thus
this imprinting will allow you to activate your very ancient
coding within you. Then when you leave you will take it with
you. You will have the ability to activate others as well.

*Who imprinted it? This was supposedly the west end of Lemuria over-
laid with the east end of Atlantis. Those energies are here. There are
space beings coming in, making use of dimensional portals. Is all of
that related to this?*

Yes. The idea of the vortexes that are considered magnetic
would be more Lemurian in nature. The vortexes that are considered electric would be more Atlantean.

Who imprinted them? What was the nature or source of the imprinting consciousness?

For the sake of the answer, we would say the consciousness you know of as the Founders. They represent a fragment of your galactic matrix.

So they deliberately created the energy field? It has always been here since the beginning of the planet?

Yes, no matter what geology existed here. The gridwork in this area was the same as now. There have been periods of time when there was latency in the energy, but that only reflected the mass consciousness at the moment.

So when it was underwater it was still there even if no one could come and use it?

It was still there. During the times it was underwater there was only a short period when it was active. Most of the time it was dormant. Right now on your planet in the last fifty of your years the energy has been reactivated in a stronger way because it will serve your mass consciousness and you as individuals greatly through your processing, integration, and activation of yourselves.

Would you say that another way of expressing that the Founders imprinted it, is that we did it in our mass-conscious oneness to sort of guide us through the fragmentation?

Yes. You, the Founders, and the Creator are one, in that sense.

So what are we activating? What old codes? Can you be specific about that? How can we facilitate or cooperate with this process?

You can cooperate with the process simply by not judging your own life. That is really what it boils down to. We cannot tell you, "If you do *this* you will activate your code immediately, you will ascend, and that will be it." No. You are part of the Earth-plane process. You are doing it for yourself, but you are also doing it for your planet. The activation that we speak of is an activation on many levels. One level is *total memory*, first of your Earth's history. From there you go to galactic memory, and then to memory of All That Is.

So it is like a timed program in a computer. It is scheduled to come on-line when something triggers it.

Yes.

What are the triggers?

It has been triggered. This is already beginning. You don't have to worry about booting it up. It has already started.

How do we become skilled at using the program?

Don't pull the plug!

I've heard that Mt. Shasta is Earth's heart-chakra vortex and Sedona is her mid-abdominal vortex.

Relationship to Earth's Chakra System

We would say there have been many, many translations of that idea. It really has to do with the reading of mass conscious-ness at any given moment. We equate Mt. Shasta with the crown chakra.

And Sedona?

We do not consider Sedona one of the *major* ones.

Hawaii would be the heart?

Yes.

So then what is the importance of Sedona as a center of energy? If there are only twelve vortexes, then how...

Only twelve *major* vortexes, like the chakras.

Then is this a major energy vortex, one of the twelve?

No. It is not one of the twelve, but at the same time it per-forms a very vital function for the individuals that partake of the energy. Understand that the planetary chakras, the main ones that were spoken of, are the main chakras for the mass con-sciousness of your planet or the planet as an entity. There need to be areas on the planet that do not necessarily serve the *entity* but which are committed to serving individuals or groups *within* the entity. Sedona is one of the vortical areas that serves individuals and groups of the entity. This is why it is such a strong area of networking. It links groups. Individuals will come here on pilgrimages in order to work on their individual self and grow to best represent the entire Earth itself. This is an energetic school.

Other than the group focus, what are other benefits from the vortexes of Sedona to the individual?

The benefits are really infinite, since each and every one of you are different. You will find that generally all of the benefits fall into the category of integration on either the mental, physical, spiritual or emotional levels. That is summing it up but not saying it all. It really depends on the individual. Truly speaking, when you come to Sedona, you will *always* get what you need. It may not necessarily be what you've asked for, but you *will* get what you need in a more accelerated and intensified way.

So Sedona is not one of the twelve major vortexes, but it has this power. Where did this energy come from? How did it get here? What is the mechanics of the source of it?

Energy Gridwork Formed Spirals

For the sake of the analogy, let us say you have a gridwork laid over the planet. In the beginning all area points on the planet were equal. There were not necessarily any that were more powerful than the others. *Consciousness* is the variable here. As consciousness began interacting with the planet, it began triggering certain areas of the planet and forming or instigating the spiraling of energy. It is like giving a heart that is not beating an electric shock to get it to beat. Once the consciousness began coming to your planet, then it began forming its own pattern and matrix.

The Sedona area began forming its vortical structure *before* the Lemurian times. When the beings started coming to your planet etherically, this was one of the first areas they began coming through.

You mean as a dimensional gateway or doorway?

Yes, and this began setting up the vortical structure.

So was their energy coming from out of the system?

Yes.

So it creates a wake almost like a boat goes through water or a plane through air?

Thank you. Yes.

And some of their high energy stayed here in this little eddy?

Yes. Eddy—very descriptive. Rather than using water as an analogy, we could use hair-setting gel. If you were to put it in a pan and flatten its surface, it would take the shape of your hand were you to lay your hand upon it. It is an *imprint.*

In the energy of this area? You mean it stays even though the Earth turns and moves?

Yes. It has been said that vortex areas may shift. Some vortexes may even neutralize. This is so, and it occurs because somehow there is a force in that gridwork of your planet powerful enough to shift the structure/imprint of the grid (or "gel"). That is how vortexes change or move.

So could that happen with Sedona?

It could, yes.

I'd like to talk about the relationship of vortexes and their qualities to the seismic nature of Earth's geology. Most major vortexes that we know of are lone mountains and thus volcanos (such as Mt. Shasta and Mt. Fuji and the twin peaks just north of us, as well as the Hawaiian islands). This area also has a high degree of seismic activity, but it is very concentrated, unlike the lone mountains.

Vortexes Allow Release of Pressure

Simply put, the areas of vortical activity allow for doorways that can bleed off the built-up energy within the Earth's structure. The idea you call seismic activity is not just a physical thing; it also exists as an ionic change as well as changes in etheric levels. It is a release of energy. Generally speaking, if you have a piece of paper with holes poked through it and you wish to release some air, the air will come through the paper where the holes are. When you have pressure in your Earth (energetically, etherically, physically) and the pressure is released, it automatically will be drawn to the areas that can funnel it out and dissipate it.

Remember that the conical structure of the vortex allows a dissipation of energy. Therefore seismic activity will "seek" vortex areas in order to be dissipated.

Mt. Shasta Energies Compared with Sedona's

In comparing Mt. Shasta with Sedona, Mt. Shasta gradually dissipates into the surrounding area. Sedona doesn't really dissipate, as far as what we can feel. It simply ends, like a very specific bubble. Why is that?

Sedona is a group of minor vortexes. When we say "minor," it is not meant as an insult. It is simply that there are *groups* of vortexes here rather than one vortex. Imagine if Sedona were just *one* vortex! You would have the most powerful vortex on the planet. It could not manifest as one vortex—the energy would be too intense.

So one reason why all of us are drawn here is the quality and the characteristics of this group of vortexes here?

Yes, and also what they can do for you.

What is the energetic difference between Sedona and Mt. Shasta and how does it relate to us?

First of all, we are going to digress from what you just asked and say that what we have just shared with you about the seismic activity and the bleed-off can also be related to the personality. What a vortex area such as Sedona can do for you is this: When you come here you allow your own inner seismic energy to be drawn to the surface and released. The vortexes draw it out of you and dissipate it. Now, ask your question again.

In comparing vortexes, can you speak of frequency, color, or rates of spin? Just use symbology.

Mt. Shasta can be considered to pulse more slowly than the minor vortexes in the Sedona area. The ones in Sedona pulse more rapidly.

Is that why they are used for more specific purposes? For instance, let's say that Shasta would have a broad spectrum of frequencies it pulsed. Does Sedona have a more narrowly focused range?

We would say just the opposite. Shasta has a more narrow range of frequency and Sedona is more broad. You are dealing with the difference between one vortex and many.

Electric, Magnetic and EM Properties

Can the vortex energy be described as electromagnetic [EM]?

It depends on which vortex you speak of.

They would have to be electromagnetic; one would be more magnetic or electric than another. Because they couldn't just be one or the other, is that true?

One will always have properties of the other, yes. It is just the balance you are asking about. Within the Sedona area, though a vortex may be labeled "electric," it will have magnetic properties. It is just that the electric properties are more pronounced.

What would induce it to be more electric or magnetic?

Initially, when the vortexes were formed, the qualities of the energy template that formed the initial vortexes imprinted them with the specific range of frequencies they would be expressing. It is the idea of placing the hand in the hair gel.

Bell Rock, for example, is somewhat conically shaped. Is that one of the reasons it generates a vortex?

No. In that specific instance, it does not matter what the shape of Bell Rock is. Bell Rock itself is not the vortex. It is the energy structure that interfaces with the coordinates of Bell Rock. If you took some dynamite and blew it to bits the vortex would still remain.

I have a question about people passing through Sedona rather than spending lifetimes here. Is it possible to overdose in the sense that the energies would become detrimental after a period of time? Or is it just that the benefit drops off?

There have been individuals who have allowed the energies to become detrimental, yes. We would say it is set up to be a pass-through point. Should someone choose to make their lives here, we would suggest that they be extremely truthful and willing to look in the mirror of their soul constantly. If you spend years here, the energy of Sedona has the ability to create illusion very strongly. You would thus begin to live in your own bubble and isolate yourself from what you'd originally chosen to do—which is to *become* the vortex and radiate it outward.

We haven't really talked about how the human body, mind, spirit and emotions react in a vortex like Sedona.

Personal Vortex Structures Entrained

If you come into Sedona for the first time in this life, more often than not you will experience a blowing out of every chakra—particularly strong in the heart, throat and third eye. Some individuals will feel this physically, some may not. It really depends on the person. What occurs is that when they place themselves in close proximity to the vortexes, their own vortex structure becomes awakened and begins to attempt a synchronized pulsing, an entrainment with the area vortexes. Some of you will notice the change immediately in the body.

Those of you who return here often will find that each time you come, this attempt to synchronize your chakras with the vortexes becomes easier and occurs perhaps without your noticing. Those of you who live here will go through periods when you are synchronized 100% with the pulses of the vortexes. There are other times when you go out of sync, and that is all right. It is a natural process. When you leave Sedona to go to another town, your body (if it is just a day) will generally retain the alignment and balance. If you leave for perhaps four days, when you come back there will be a slight realignment.

What does it feel like when you are out of sync with the vortexes here?

It can manifest physically, emotionally, spiritually, or mentally. Generally it is somewhat a level of confusion. Mental confusion would be the feeling of being unable to follow your thought patterns. Emotionally, you would experience many reactions for no apparent reason. Spiritually, perhaps you may feel a weight, a doubt of your own process. Physically, it can manifest as all sorts of ailments that really have no cause.

If someone is experiencing this, being out of balance, probably in denial (in a big way)—they could quite easily get off on some paranoid track, like being bombarded with ELF waves or something.

They could become paranoid, yes.

So it could be their own denial or lack of alignment?

It could be, yes. It is not a complete yes, but it *could* be that individuals might allow themselves to become paranoid, even schizophrenic.

If a person chooses to live here but travels constantly, does that assist in balancing out the whole situation?

Yes. Further, it assists in the person bringing that energy to other places and dispersing it from himself. You don't ever lose it.

Would you say that these vortexes have a tendency to affect individual chakras?

Yes. We will not make a comparison or equate various chakras with vortexes, because vortexes will activate various chakras, not just one. What we will do is talk about the main vortexes in Sedona and the colors and the chakras that you may use to *maximize* the energy there.

Sedona Vortex/Chakra/Color Correlations

Let us start with **Airport Vortex**. If you wish to go to that particular vortex, you may work with the base chakra (red), the second chakra (orange), and the solar-plexus chakra (yellow). Also, you may work with the throat chakra (blue).

If you go to **Red Rock Crossing/Cathedral Rock** to maximize the energy there, you may wish to work with the heart chakra (pink and green). You may also work with the second chakra (orange), which is sexuality, the third-eye chakra (indigo), and the crown (violet).

At **Bell Rock** you may work with the third-eye chakra (indigo), the crown (violet), the throat (blue), and the solar plexus (yellow).

In **Boynton Canyon** you may work with the heart chakra (green and pink), the base chakra (red), the second chakra (orange) of sexuality, and the third eye (indigo).

In the area you call **Montezuma's Well** you may work with the heart chakra (green) and the third eye (indigo).

In the area you call **Long Canyon** you may work with the base chakra (red) and the solar plexus (yellow).

At the area you call **Schnebly Hill** you may work with the solar plexus and the heart (greenish yellow). This specific area represents, more than any other, the transformation from third to fourth density.

In the **San Francisco Peaks** area you may work with the crown chakra (violet) and the third eye (indigo).

We wish to state here that these are malleable. What we have given you are ways to *maximize* the energy in any given area. You may use any color and any chakra. This is just our perception of the maximization of energy.

But these are just the lower chakras. What about the other five?

The other chakra areas would be more equated with the etheric points that do not exist within time and space. In that sense, we have left them out, since you would have no reference point. Do you follow?

No. They are very real. One couldn't focus on any of them?

Yes, you could. We have said only that this is a *maximization* of energy within the body and the Earth. If you find that you wish to work with any of the upper chakras in these physical areas, we would leave that up to you.

One is not better than any of the others?

No.

What about West Fork?

We would say that the **West Fork** energy, should you wish to maximize it, can be used with the crown chakra (violet). You can also, if you wish, use the upper chakras 8 through 12. It is outside the basic perimeter of Sedona. It is not so intense, but much more healing.

Could we generalize that Sedona, being red, is more activating to our lower chakras?

In that sense you can say that Sedona represents the red and the violet—a joining of the Earth and the heavens.

In terms of vortex energy in these different spots, could you say that the vortex energy at Airport is primarily at the top of the mountain or in the saddle area, or is there some specific location where the energy would be the highest?

When you park your car below the mesa and walk up the hill to the east toward the saddle, you will get to the lip [where it drops into the canyon]. When you do this you reach the outer perimeter of **Airport Vortex**. As you go down into the canyon itself, you approach the more condensed aspects of the vortex. That vortex radiates outward, touching most of the mesa itself.

What about the others, like Bell Rock? Where would one go to maximize it?

Bell Rock would be the rock itself. You will feel the vibrations of the vortex from the very base. The more you climb it (because it is shaped somewhat conically), the closer you get to the core of the spiral at its top.

You will find that **Cathedral Rock** itself is the emanation of the vortex. The energy there radiates for miles.

If you could climb to the point of the spire, would that be the highest energy?

Actually, the point called "the black pyramid" would be more akin to the peak of energy. The black pyramid is below the spires. If you see it in person or look at a picture, there is a rock formation that resembles a pyramid structure that is black or grey in color.

What about Schnebly? Is it along the road?

Schnebly Hill is another area in Sedona not considered one of the major vortexes, but an area of energy that radiates perhaps within a two-mile diameter, the center point being approximately two miles from the beginning of the unpaved road.

So it is two miles up that road as you drive a car. That would be the center?

Roughly. Understand that the centers are not always right there on the road!

Where would be the maximal use of energy in Boynton Canyon?

It depends on what you wish to use the **Boynton Canyon** energy for, or what you wish to stimulate within yourself. If you wish a feminine interaction, we would suggest the path that leads deeper into the wooded part. The temperature drops, and it has a very different feel to it after walking for a bit. The path would be to the left when you park your car. If you wish to experience a more masculine idea, we would suggest you move into the canyon itself, as far into the center of it as you can.

Would you consider Boynton the major vortex area in Sedona?

No. To state which area is the major vortex area would depend on your definition of a major vortex area.

I've heard that Airport Vortex has some ancient feminine energy. Is this so?

In the ancient Lemurian times, slightly after the waters receded, that area around **Airport Vortex** was the home of a great warrioress. So in that area there is a feminine energy masculinely expressed.

What about the "chakra-blowing" potential?

That is all we needed! Thank you. Chakra-blowing potential! They are neck-and-neck for number one—Bell Rock and Airport. Airport is running a close first, Bell Rock a nose behind, as you say. The others exist within a spectrum that is very similar. Those two stand out.

Did these vortex areas also function as entrances to other dimensions or inner Earth?

Dimensional Portals

This was addressed by Sasha, but we will say that they can at times. Most of the portals are not stationary. They do move around. The primary access for portals exists within the Boynton and Long Canyon areas. There can be entrances in the Bell Rock area for extraterrestrial consciousness.

How would you access those?

They will not be accessed at this time unless it is absolutely imperative for you to do so.

Is there a physical access to inner Earth at Airport? I was told very specifically there was, and given specific directions.

Have you found it?

No.

Have you looked?

A little bit.

It is our perception that the closest entrance point to inner Earth from Sedona exists in Mt. Shasta—physically, no portals involved.

Is it at the top of the mountain?

Not at the top, but perhaps halfway up.

Is it being used?

Yes. There are some humans that know about it and use it.

What do they do when they get inside?

Very few have found the [extraterrestrial] base beneath, which exists within fourth density. It is a base for the Association of Worlds (a positive group). Some have seen this. Most who venture far enough will find that they conveniently fall asleep or experience missing time. Some have had hypnosis to find out what experiences occurred during the missing time. These experiences are of an extraterrestrial nature. Most people that venture in get tired long before they reach anything. It is, as you say, a long walk.

If Mt. Shasta represents an entrance to inner Earth, what would Sedona vortex energy represent? Entrance to what—ET energy or something?

It represents a doorway for extraterrestrial consciousness to *enter* your Earth plane—one of the major ones. Also, understand the idea of entrances and exits. Sometimes entrances cannot be used as exits, and exits cannot be used as entrances. So in that sense, sometimes you will find that Sedona can be used as *exit* points from the inner Earth, but not back in.

Is there a particular place in West Fork, like a mile marker on the way up the canyon?

The turnout on the right [east side] of the road is where you would park. You would enter there and walk in approximately one and one-half miles. Again, the point will not be right there along the path.

Does Secret Canyon represent a vortex area?

Secret Canyon and Andromedans

It represents, in a sense only, a neutral or buffer zone. It does utilize the vortex energy but can be used as a neutral zone, which is why some extraterrestrial consciousnesses can enter through that area.

Are they currently using Secret Canyon as an entrance to the Earth plane?

Yes. Primarily at this time that we speak, it is used by Andromedan consciousness.

Is this through interaction as UFOs?

They are interdimensional, curious beings. They are travelers, tourists, and intergalactic peacekeepers.

Who are they keeping the peace from?

It is to protect you from various energies they perceive are attempting infiltration—what you consider negative extraterrestrial consciousness.

If they came here as fourth-dimensional beings, they could see clearly everything in the third dimension, but we couldn't see them? Could they walk around in their etheric bodies and see us in detail?

Yes. Depending, though, upon their specific frequency orientation, they may need to screen out various frequencies in your reality that may become painful for them.

Granted that they could do that, they could walk up and down the street and see us, and we couldn't see them?

If they want to be seen, they will densify. If they do not, they won't.

So when they cannot be seen, it is not like they are in a different dimension and we are all blurry. They can see us precisely in detail?

Well, to you it would seem blurry, because they would also see auric fields. You will seem like an energy pattern, much more complete than you see yourselves.

So they are not limited to the mere physical shell. They see all of the bodies at one time.

Correct. But they do have the ability to be selective in what they see. If they wish to see only your auric field, they can tune out your physical body. If they wish to see only the physical body, they can tune out the auric field. It is the same idea as your being in a room and shutting out the background noise to listen to a conversation.

If a group of Indians or Lemurians ascended from a specific spot and I stood there, would that energy affect me at this time? Would it still be resonant?

It would affect you if it would assist you in experiencing whatever process in your life you were going through at that moment. If you experienced everything that ever occurred in the same time/space you were standing in, your senses would literally be overloaded. There is a selective sensitization.

Are there places within this area with that ascension energy that would be beneficial to go to?

We would say that the closest thing in this area to what you would consider ascension energy would be the Twin Peaks, the San Francisco Peaks.

At the top?

Yes, although you can glean the experience somewhat from being at the base and projecting yourself emotionally to the top.

In terms of the general Sedona vortex energy, can we use a geometric shape to additionally enhance the energy already present here?

Geometric Shapes to Enhance Different Vortexes

Yes. Sedona represents many different energies. In the Cathedral Rock area, we would consider a dome to be useful in enhancing the energy. In Boynton Canyon it would be a dome or pyramid. At Bell Rock, the conical shape or a three-sided pyramid. At Airport Vortex we would suggest a conical shape.

The conical shape is essentially a teepee. The Indians who used them were obviously aware of this energy. Do they actually use these for spiritual purposes?

Initially the teepee was created as a representational understanding of the universal vortex idea. Later they began utilizing them as dwellings in order to bring that energy to Earth.

Would it be possible to actually harness this energy that radiates out of the focal point of the cone in any third-dimensional way?

You can *simulate* it using magnetics, not harness it.

It creates a magnetic condition?

Spinning magnets can *simulate* the idea of creating a cone or vortex pattern of energy.

Conversely, then, there would be a magnetic condition or anomaly created at the focal point of a cone or pyramid?

Yes.

Can this be harnessed in some way that we can use?

In third-dimensional/density reality you can only *simulate* it. You will not harness the actual vortical energy itself, because it is interdimensional.

Can we harness it psychically then?

Yes, but not in its entirety.

What kind of energy is between vortexes, like in normal places?

Generally you will have either neutral zones, buffer zones (which are two different things), or two different dissipated frequencies rubbing against each other. You will have pure energy and you will have overlapping energy from the vortexes. In the Sedona area you will not be in calm waters. There are points in outlying areas that can be considered calm waters. Sasha has pointed out the neutral zone outside Sedona. There is generally a wave form here or there somewhere in Sedona.

Are they like eddies?

Yes. They are like currents, eddies, riptides in some places. They do not necessarily cycle in a circular pattern.

Sasha talked about the nexus points that went through the Earth, which I assumed were these twelve major vortexes. They were at the intersection of the grid lines. So Sedona does not have grid intersections with the nexus points?

Correct.

Sedona doesn't have nexus points that go through the Earth or deeply into the Earth. These are formed, as you said, by these beings who created this area, which is an acceleration point.

We would say that the primary vortexes in Sedona *do* touch the center of the Earth. We would not consider Sedona to be a primary vortex area simply because of the definitions that are assigned to the primary vortex areas—which have one consistent pulsation. That is what makes Sedona different from a major vortex area—it does not have one consistent pulsation.

Ah, but other than that, it has the qualities of a major Earth vortex?

Basically speaking, you will find that a major vortex area on your planet will have either a very calming or a very distressing effect on you. In Sedona you can combine that. So in that sense, it doesn't fall in line with the definition of the major vortexes as being one *concise* pulsation.

Is there a direction of rotation for vortexes?

In Sedona you will find it to be generally counterclockwise.

Thank you. We send our love as always. We express to you how we see you, which is always as the brightest of stars. Never forget how bright your flames burn. Goodnight.

6

More Questions Answered

Bearclaw and Zoosh
Through Robert Shapiro
Channeled 3/11/90

What is the precise dynamic or mechanics that happens when a human being with an energy field goes into a vortex? What is the process?

Auric Molecules Charged

BEARCLAW: From my understanding, the molecular structure of the human is altered only from the instant that they actually *feel* the effect. When they feel the change, they can have a moment of expanding into their auric density and actually be *in* it. In other words, an expanded consciousness occurs on a molecular level. The molecules in your auric field are charged considerably greater than they are charged now, so they become radiating sources as well as receiving sources. The change that happens in consciousness is largely due to the interaction of the neurons, and brain chemicals are involved in the speeding up of this auric exchange.

When exposed to this nurturing magnetic energy, one tends to explode, in a sense, into a greater, speeded-up energy of the auric field. The emanations of your auric field allow physiological changes in that moment that will stimulate thoughts, inspirations, aspirations of spirit that can be aligned to a life that is practical and grounded, since this emanation is coming from the Earth itself. And there are also potentials to reach much higher levels of expression of the heart.

What about the people that live in the town and don't go to individual vortexes? Is there an energy in the town, or do you physically have to go to the vortexes to get the effects?

It is better to go directly to the areas. The energy of the town now has more individuals occupying the space, which becomes involved with the hurly-burly of daily life and has little to do with the focusing of energy. When one makes a trip to these holy sites—sacred sites with spirit and desire and need and offerings—sometimes a dance is an offering, because you must make the effort. You must show that you have desires and needs; you must do something in order to receive something. Sometimes when you go to these places you experience the full effect; you get to use the dance, because your auric field has been filled with yourself. When you ask for these things in town, they may come, but they will come quicker in these other areas. Always ask for that which feeds you and does not do injury to others, for any request—mark my words—of injury done to others will surely come back upon yourself.

What does it mean to have a vortex? Where does the energy come from? What keeps it there?

Stimulation, Transformation and Extragalactic Communication

It is a functioning element of Earth designed to send messages to soul consciousnesses that exist in other galaxies and in the Earth Mother's auric field. It sends invitations to come to this area to exist and perform here in some way in order to feed or sustain this area.

It is also an energy designed to transform. *All* of the vortexes are designed to transform—that is why it is not possible to live there. In order to have a consistent life, one must do certain things the same way. One must often take a cup of water and place it to the lips to drink. How does one transform such a basic act? This is why we do not encourage people to live directly in the vortex areas here. There has been some encouragement of these areas. However, those areas do not always fare very well, since the encroachment can really be successfully done only by those who are aware of the purpose of the vortex. So I will say that the function is designed to change, to stimulate, and to call.

Who or what designed them?

Vortexes in Humans

That which is the Creator designs that for all places. Do you know that the human being also has vortexes? Not just in the chakra areas, but also at times in other areas, sometimes in the hand. If you've had a handshake that is indecisive or inconclusive, that is a vortex projecting somewhat out as, "Get away, I don't really want you." But maybe there will be a magnetic vortex, one that is pulling you toward it. You feel the handshake and it is strong and firm. It says, "Welcome. I've been waiting for you. I'm happy to see you."

Human beings are simply images of the Earth Mother. The Earth Mother is an image of the Creator's imagination, as are all planets, all bodies, all consciousnesses, and every thing.

Other Vortex Areas

Are there other areas on the Earth like these vortexes in Sedona?

There are many, many areas. There are a few vortexes that project. Some of them call. This area primarily calls. The area referred to as the Bermuda Triangle also calls. It calls people—only those who need to go elsewhere, for it is a dimensional changer. It is a doorway. Those who are not called and pass through the area, pass through safely and arrive at their destination. Those who are called and must be elsewhere simply disappear into that other realm.

There are other areas that send. In northern Tibet there is an area that sends. It is not calling for people to come. It is constantly sending information and energy. It sends the frequency dynamic energy of the entire total experience of the surface and the inner Earth to the Creator and to the Creator's representatives so that all will know what is needed and what is becoming here on this planet.

What is your perception of what happens to a divine light encapsulated in a human body when it goes into a vortex area? What are the dynamics?

How a Vortex Affects Humans

ZOOSH: I understand you would like a mechanical explanation. Essentially, the human being can come into spiritual alignment simply by laughing! You do not have to be extremely emotional. You can be motion as being in e-motion. Recognize that *motion* is a factor involved in experiencing the ultimate aspect of the vortex.

The vortex will allow you to experience every single incarnation that you have ever had anywhere. In other words, you will sometimes have new skills and abilities upon exiting because you will pick them up and draw them to you from your previous parallel or probable future incarnations. This is why people can be changed by the experience. Equally, one could conceivably lose interest in someone or something.

Know that the experience in the vortex is to be used reverentially, that is to say, not casually. If you are having a fight with your buddy, pal, lover, wife, husband, children, that is *not* a really good time to run to a vortex, because then you'd often be looking for an escape, and you might find it in a life that was disinterested in this soul that you are connecting with.

So know that vortexes are to be used to gain from all of your previous and potential past and future lives. I will give you that rather than giving the mechanics of how it works, because the mechanics of how it works is dull. It is essentially a *supermicrobiological interaction* with organisms that function beyond the level of physical biology.

Sonic Vibrations Create Change

Imagine the ultimate ray, the ultimate vibration. Imagine the lowest vibration. All of the tones that go beyond the scale into sonics and ultrasonics can be accessed there. What occurs is largely the mingling and commingling of these ultrasonic, ultrahigh, ultralow, ultradense, ultrathin aspects, all interacting with your microbiological structure within your body, auric field, and imagination to change *if change is desired.* So, *know* what you want before you go into a vortex, because it is possible to feel uncomfortable after you leave. If you have been feeling self-destructive, for example, don't go there.

From your perception, how are the vortexes formed?

You are asking how life is formed! It is by the Creator. It is *before* time, before space, before this planet existed. If you took this planet out of this space, the vortexes would *still* be there because they are performing a function.

Why Some Don't Feel Vortex Energies

Why is it that some people don't seem to have a reaction to the vortexes and others do?

In the case of a personified will—in other words, when an individual is living primarily by the motivations of his mind and his feeling is perhaps encapsulated closer to his body— there may not be any reaction. In another case, an individual may have been here long enough or have been exposed to such energies long enough that it is not necessary to come here to experience those energies. One can experience as the *microcosmic self* within one's own body any of those energies that can be experienced in Sedona. Also, if you have had a sufficient exposure you might not feel it. You might not notice it, yet it does take place.

So understand that not feeling it does not necessarily mean that there is nothing taking place. It depends largely upon where your aura is. When you desire something, when you seek something—even the explorer seeking to see what the next canyon looks like—you are sending out a great deal of your energy. You are essentially a bigger target. Then the enveloping energy fields can interact with more of you. When you are compacted, it is understood then that the desire is not there necessarily to change, but to simply be. That is respected.

Could you explain why some people get very weak and sick to their stomach in the vortexes?

Feeling Ill in a Vortex

If you are aware of what you are thinking, feeling, and desiring, the safest way to exist in any vortex is to be in motion at all times. Think about it. It is not a good place to sleep, all right? It is not a good place to have disagreements with people. Be aware of your actual motivations. It is a place to become *aware* of your motivations. Sometimes you are driven by forces that you do not understand. In a vortex these things will come to the surface. On one hand you may say, "Well, that is good, Zoosh, because they are being processed." Yet on the other hand one might simply say, "I can think of more comfortable ways to process."

The vortex will bring your subconscious energy to the surface without including your mind in it. No one goes into a vortex, even at the outer perimeters, without having their subconscious affected. The vortex interacts with all aspects of you —your unconscious, your subconscious and your conscious mind, but it does not interfere with the process of learning how to become a human being. So you've got to become aware of your unconscious and your subconscious, for it is all there to be accessed.

A vortex can interact with all of that, you understand? A vortex does not in its own right have an unconscious or subconscious. It has only an awareness of being. Therefore it is going to access all levels of you. Be aware of this when you go into a vortex. Bring only that which is comfortable transformation to you now. And keep moving. When you get tired, sit down— but sort of move around.

A Vortex As Consciousness

So there is an intelligence or consciousness within the vortex itself?

Certainly! It is in many senses alive. What is the definition of life? You tell me. I will wait.

It is consciousness...It is awareness...To experience feelings...Love... Change...Evolution.

Thank you. All very good definitions. They exist within the vortex because the vortex seeks, it follows, it allows, it becomes, it receives. It exists as a form and function of the Creator. One might say there is even a devic energy, a consciousness associated with all vortexes everywhere.

In terms of our transitioning from third to fourth dimension, is there a particular place in Sedona that would help facilitate that?

The Greatest Energy Bombardment

You can really go any place on Earth, since the entire planet is transitioning. But if you want to go someplace and spread out and be *bombarded* by the energies that are radiating, get directly on *top* of Bell Rock, spreadeagle yourself, and you can be bombarded! However, that may not be the most comfortable thing to do.

Are you saying that it is better not to meditate on the vortexes? That we should stay moving instead?

Moving Meditations Best

It is all right to meditate, but *move* as you meditate. Consider that meditation need not be something that uses thought to stimulate feeling. It is better to *be in motion* in the vortexes, much better. You can do a meditation that requires interaction with your environment, even if it is going back and forth between two trees that you particularly like, or two rocks. A vortex is not a place I recommend for meditation, in terms of stillness. It can be done if you can focus into the heart and areas such as this that support you. Communicate with your heart. Talk to it, "Heart, what do you want?" But I do not necessarily recommend stillness unless you can maintain a complete alignment and balance.

I am not necessarily saying that some horrible thing will come from the sky or that the kachina of the lightning will hurl a lightning bolt into your eyes if you are meditating and are not completely in touch with the goal of that meditation. However, meditations are confronted by the challenges of distraction, which are what can keep one from a truly fulfilled meditation.

The vortex, although it supports that meditation, will also support the distraction. So a vortex does not have a right and wrong; it just provides, stimulates, or activates whatever is present. So I am not saying, "Don't." What I *am* trying to do is urge you to be a little more in motion when you are in those energy areas.

ET Bases

Do the extraterrestrials use any of the Sedona vortexes as a base?

Certainly under Bell Rock. Anyone who's been around Bell Rock at night knows that. And also a couple of others in the area that I won't mention due to the highly sensitive nature of what they are doing. It can be seen from time to time in various glowing lights. That is all I will say. I will also say that there is a very powerful one near the Superstition Mountains [east of Phoenix].

That is protected from humans? How is that done?

Certain energies are radiated that will cause discomfort, distraction, or deflection. That is to say, one might become much more disoriented in the area of the Superstition Mountains than one might experience in another place.

Who is there? Can you say?

That is provided by the Creator due to what is buried there.

Are the extraterrestrials that are in the Sedona area part of the Ashtar Command?

No.

Where are they from?

They are from Arcturus, Andromeda. There are some negative ones as well, which are not of much influence. They are from the star systems you refer to astronomically as Capricornus and the Crab Nebula.

Does the Ashtar Command have a base in Arizona?

I have discussed the Ashtar "Request" on previous occasions. I will simply say that at this time those individuals who believe that that is a reality may be fervently supported in that belief; and I will say that Ashtar himself is in training to build planets.

Why do I not call it the "Command?" Because Ashtar needs to learn that requesting sometimes works better.

Are those star systems and planets you mentioned that interact with Sedona humanoid?

ET Appearances

Some of them are not humanoid. Some of them are beyond what you would refer to as any resemblance to human. This often gives them an advantage, since the interdimensional quality of their life allows them to appear somewhat two-dimensional. That is to say, a two-dimensional being would be someone who when facing you could be seen, but when turning to the side would no longer be there.

What would we see if we faced them?

An energy body that would appear to be round and very small.

How are plants and animals affected that live in vortex areas?

Plants and Animals Are Representative

Interesting question. The plants are of the highest nature. Bearclaw referred to ceremonies that would encourage the plants. What he did *not* say is that the plants that are here are representatives of those who exist elsewhere. In other words, they are the highest spirits. This is why certain native cultures have encouraged you *not* to take out the plants and to be careful with nature. Because these are like the United Nations; they are representatives of other plants. Some of them are representatives for hundreds or even thousands of species that cannot be present simply due to the weather and environment.

The animals are also representatives. They interact with the vortex energy much more excessively than a human being might because there is no resistance. There is no false personality. There is no subconscious motivation. They are exactly as they appear to be. One could perhaps see in a plant or an animal the moment when it is sending information to all other species—that moment of extreme stillness. Have you ever been in an area where there is a lot of wind and it suddenly stops and then springs up again. In that moment of stillness the trees and vegetation send out their message through representational light of the finest and highest of the Creator. They will send it to all other forms of life like themselves or relations of same. Thank you for your contributions.

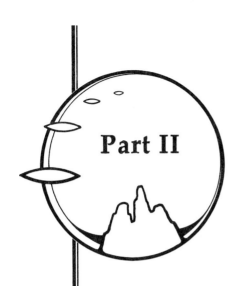

Part II

ANCIENT AND
FUTURE HISTORY

This map, though not drawn to scale, is reproduced here because it is the one upon which Vywamus, through Janet McClure, marked the sites he describes in this chapter. On page 114 is a professional rendering of this map.

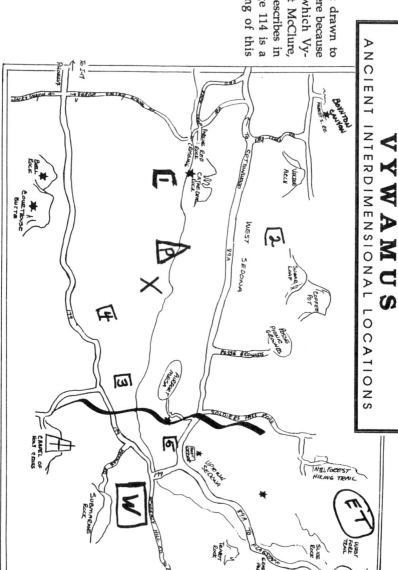

VYWAMUS

ANCIENT INTERDIMENSIONAL LOCATIONS

7

The Ancient Past and Its Traces

Vywamus Through Janet McClure
Channeled 2/19/90

I have often talked about Lemuria and Atlantis, and I have told humanity that these were not the earliest times on your planet. For a long time, however, the doorway was sealed to what occurred before Lemuria. That era, which I have called pre-Lemuria, was a difficult period, because it was a time when humanity was engaged in a 500-year war with a race of beings from another planet. After this period a new beginning occurred that was called Lemuria, which lasted for a very long time. Because of the war, much of the rather sophisticated civilization that had been present on your Earth—quite technological and quite dense in population—had been destroyed. Thus a simplistic approach to Earth living was begun again in Lemuria.

Many of you lived in caves. Although you knew how to build, there was perhaps not the desire then, for there was still a belief in vulnerability because of the recent war. Thus you confined your lives for awhile to survival, although you enjoyed decorating the beautiful caves in which you resided. You were rather mobile, moving from place to place upon the planet. Gradually, over long periods of time you began to trust again, constructing small villages and developing the beginnings of civilization once more.

An Occupation Lasting 400,000 Years

In the Sedona area there was just such a beginning civilization in the Lemurian time. You came together, having renewed your faith in life, beginning to trust again, and you built up quite a good civilization. It was a forerunner of what would occur in the Atlantean era, and it lasted into that later era. The civilization in Sedona, spiritual in nature and quite lovely, endured for approximately four hundred thousand years. One reason the energies are so strong is because of many spiritual events that have happened here.

The civilization here was, in a sense, an overlap between the Atlantean and the earlier pre-Lemurian experience. These civilizations were global in nature. There was certainly a place called Mu, and in my opinion Mu and Lemuria were the same thing, except that Mu was a physical place in the same way that Atlantis was a physical place. But there were global civilizations built around those specific physical locations. There were beings who, late in the Lemurian civilization, trusted going into the Sedona area and building up a rather idealistic spiritual community. The community remained there during the ensuing Atlantean civilization.

Early Atlantis was not very different from latter Lemuria. One literally ran into the other. But the very nature of the spiritual community in Sedona allowed an overlap between the two civilizations. We could say that the center of the government in Lemuria was in the land of Mu. The center of the government in Atlantis was in the physical continent of Atlantis itself. Also, for awhile in Lemuria you were less a part of the stars—meaning there weren't as many extraterrestrials that visited the Earth. Yes, there were some contacts, but not as many as previously and not as many as later in Atlantis—and certainly not as many as during the later Egyptian civilization.

Extraterrestrial Mining Colony

There was a time long ago when your planet received an asteroid that was then broken up on the planet. Parts of it broke up on contact and landed near Sedona. A mining development was centered here to mine this asteroid. Certain minerals were broken down through extraterrestrial technology, and some of the waste material was stacked up around the area, some as far south as Phoenix. The waste material was purposefully placed to help with the flooding that occurred here then. It had been a sea in the distant past at that time. This is a very old, very ancient area.

The interesting part was that the beings who did the mining were not all from this dimension. A dimensional door (1) is indicated on the map [see page 86] near Cathedral Rock by a three-sided box open on the right. It is a doorway through which beings came to supervise the mining in this area. They were from a system different from the one in the eleventh dimension. They used the area to access some of the rare minerals that assisted them in *their* dimension. They took them out of this area, knowing that many of the minerals originated from this asteroid. They were delighted to find these rare minerals, for in this area of Sedona you had a few natural minerals, but not many in comparison to the rich harvest they gathered from the asteroid.

An Ascension Center, Past and Future

Back in early Atlantis a group lived in the Sedona area who were extremely spiritual beings. There were several mass ascensions in the area, and these ascensions really formed some of the vortexes that are here now. Although there are many causes for vortexes, one cause is an ascension process where beings drop their burdens, the programming they've had. The movement from their light progression begins a flow of energy that later becomes a vortex.

Because there have been a number of mass ascensions in Sedona, a number of temples, a number of spiritual endeavors—some much larger than any of you know—Sedona is destined to be the home of such a temple in the future. Because of this it draws in a column of light that goes clear to the center of the Earth energy.

Present on the earth are a number of points destined to be temple centers. They certainly have been such in the past and they are going to be again in the future. They are, of course, points of eternal Nowness within the Plan. Therefore we could say that the past, the present and the future come together at these points.

An Underground Crystal City

One of the most important things that I would like to talk about is the crystal city that lies under Sedona. It is roughly in the shape of the city itself, although perhaps a little more compact than the current city limits. I have placed a violet X right at what I would consider to be an extremely important point within this crystal city.

There was a time on the Earth when humanity left the surface. They did some mining and some carving. (There is a connection with extraterrestrials and mining.) In this case, there were Earth beings who, in connection with some from other planets, carved out a beautiful city. Now, of course it wasn't done with the type of technology that is used now. There were rods of power and light vehicles that carved out vast rooms and vast areas underneath the Sedona area.

An energy resource system was installed. This was really very early in your planet's history. There were many who seemed to be threatening the surface of your planet. These were beings from several other planets. So humanity, in connection with some from other planets trying to help humanity, prepared a place where they could not only stay but where their energy resources could be built up. And the power area of Sedona was chosen. It was chosen because of the tremendous amount of energy processing that goes on there.

Within the crystal city is a place where what I will call several alternate realities come together. A centering of several possibilities is made about 450 feet below where the X is on the map. There are elevators. They are not usable at this time, but they are there and they are not too far from where I have placed the X. Will humanity find them? Possibly. It certainly is possible they might. Whether they will recognize them, I don't know.

A Temple Beautiful

Within this crystal city are particular power-rejuvenation points. People came to this area to escape the surface and what was going on there. They also came from other dimensions and other realities for rejuvenation and the balancing of their energy bodies. It was, then, a refuge like a Temple Beautiful where people could come.

Along with the transformational points within the city are large areas where bodies were stored. These were used as burial chambers with the thought that these bodies could be kept so that they could later be brought back to life. Thus, there are bodies in the area that have not decayed which the people who left them are hoping to bring back. There are approximately 400 of these bodies stored within the crystal city at this time. They are perfectly preserved because of the strength of the energy. No decay has taken place because they are supported not only by this reality, but six other alternate realities.

This area is also several hundred feet below the surface, but I am not sure that any of you would want to find it. It is certainly possible that humanity will discover it sometime. In my opinion, if a child of Light wishes to use one of those bodies, it wouldn't be too difficult because they are perfectly preserved in every way.

ET and Alternate-Reality Technologies

Also within the crystal city (and this is what I think some of you will want to look for sometime) are the technologies from several other planets and alternate realities. They have many clues for you in your technological advancement. In point of fact, when you are able to find these, I know you will be ready for those next steps, which this crystal city can put you in touch with.

There are waves of energy that broadcast from this city, and to get in touch with them you can go to any of the major power points and ask to be aware of the crystal city and its layout. You can then get the parameters of the area. It is large, as I've said, and contains all sorts of buildings and records. Many of these records are on a type of crystal and stored with a crystal technology, so that by attuning to the crystal and then finding the whereabouts of the crystal city, you will once again learn about the technology of crystals.

I hope that people who read this won't dig up all of Sedona to find it. I would say that in the lines of probability there will be a small group very pure of heart that eventually finds this and is dedicated to helping humanity, not looking for self-glorification or power through this discovery.

8

Ancient and Future Civilizations

Zoosh Through Robert Shapiro
Channeled 3/11/90

There are very ancient civilizations that have lived in Sedona. Perhaps the most ancient civilization is one that will live here once again. Now, the souls of Earth—those who have manifested here before and those who will manifest again—have chosen this area and a few others to re-form a city that will be mostly under water. You have noticed, perhaps, that some of the rock formations seem to be residual, or leftovers of some aquatic culture. In time some of the creatures that you know as aquatic animals will be there again: dolphins, whales, some sea turtles. But that will be many, many years in the future.

A Future Resurrected Civilization

The civilization I am referring to is associated with the *underground* civilization of Lemuria—not the surface civilization that fought many discomforting challenges with Atlantis. They lived under the seas and did not cohabit with the surface population. The aspect of Lemuria some refer to as Mu might be the most appropriate title for those who will live here again.

This ancient Lemurian culture is very advanced and has left rods of power in some of the areas referred to as the vortexes. They are set to a timing that is based upon Earth's energy field. The sampling will take place when Mother Earth is no longer shielding and protecting you from interfacing with other races—meaning that you have moved to your fourth-dimensional aspect and Earth is beginning to come into a wetter cycle. When all the polar icecaps have melted, allowing the underground waters to come forth and flood the Earth so that only the highest mountains will surface, then will come those beings from that little planet in Sirius with very negative energy. They will become aquatic beings who live in and under the surface of the waters. They will inherit the cycle of Mu.

In a divine timing the rains and floods will be allowed to come when the human being has moved into its fourth-dimensional aspect and when the inheritor civilization from Sirius arrives here in the distant future. It is true that this civilization has been living in a negative surrounding; yet when they inherit the planet, they will be allowed to have both positivity and negativity such as yourselves, and live in the third dimension and become aquatic like many of their brothers and sisters in the galaxy [system] of Sirius.

This is their evolution, you see. They will be surrounded by creatures associated with Sirius, such as the dolphins, whales, sea turtles and others. Understand that this area is being prepared for them even now, and those tuning rods will know when to begin to prepare the area. That will be after you have left and exist on the fourth-dimensional aspect of this planet that I refer to as Terra and when the others are ready to arrive and undergo their change. The rods will know this by sampling the auric field of Mother Earth, which looks somewhat like a figure eight with Earth in the center where the two veins cross. The vortexes here are simply a part of that field.

The Cyclic Civilization of Mu

Mu is a civilization and is cyclical in intent. Since this Sedona area is also cyclical, as Bearclaw explains, the inherited cultures will thus be able to survive. Mu is a civilization that functions on music, sound, and constant interaction with its environment. It has been known on the surface as a place of dance and love. There is a form of dance that is motion through water; yet it has a constant awareness of both pleasure and danger around it.

Since these beings will be coming here from that mostly negative place and will be constantly aware of danger, they will be frightened of this new environment and their new bodies, which will be aquatic in appearance—that is, with webbed hands and feet to allow easy motion through the water. They will be supported with pleasures as well, since they will be living with aquatic creatures and given certain built-in tools that will allow them to feel safe. They will become more interactive with their environment. They will feel safe because they will have almost a crustacean appearance, structures around their bodies that will allow them to feel quite safe interacting in their environment. An individual will feel safe alone; it will be a lesson in safety for them.

These beings will cycle into the Mu energy while you cycle beyond it. They are inheriting the Mu energy because those from Mu who have cycled through it are not only the shamans, but those who have come to be known as kahunas. The Huna religion stems from and is sourced in Mu (in association with this planet Earth) and in Sirius (its origin).

I have given you an idea of what is coming here. Now I must give you an idea of what has been.

Power Struggles of the Past

In the past there have been largely power struggles, since this area is highly charged magnetically and equally charged positively (that is, it can push or it can pull). It has been the source of struggles, but not so much among the recent native populations, who understood that it was holy ground designed for personal and tribal transformation. It was the ancient cultures that fought over it, because it could be used as a power or energy source, a healing source—and for those who were in struggle, it could also be used as a weapon.

Now, it is possible (and has been done in the past) to use vortex energy as a weapon. One might say that the weapon was generally used positively, by deflecting meteors, asteroids or satellites of one sort or another, thus preventing them from crashing into Earth at a time when Earth's gravitational field and atmosphere were not so powerful as deflectors. There needed to be something that could deflect bodies of solid mass that might strike the planet. It is possible to focus a vortex energy into a very small mass and utilize it either as an attracting force of tremendous power or, in the case of other vortexes, a force that pushes things away or moves them into a different arc around a planet.

Your own moon was attracted to this planet by ancient previous cultures. This moon, though it appeared to be of a form and function similar to this immediate planet, was originally associated with Mars. Those who explore Mars will discover that the minerals on Mars are identical to the minerals on the moon. This will confuse them to some extent, because they have already found on the moon some minerals that have no apparent function or form on planet Earth.

Destruction of the Earth's Binary Moon

I suggest to you that the vortexes have been abused. Why was the moon attracted away from Mars, and was Mars able to afford the loss of the moon at that time? The struggles that occurred in past ancient civilizations were so great, and one particular civilization desired to destroy its enemies so intensely, that it was willing essentially to commit suicide and so destroyed Earth's binary moon. There was a moon here then that had an equal and opposite moon, which is why the planet is a little warped.

Those of you who are hobbyists in physics (or even physicists) may be acquainted with this material and know that the Earth is not exactly round. This is because of the gravitational effect of a *binary* moon that once existed around this planet—that is to say, two equal and opposite asteroids, equal in terms of mass, structure, shape, form. They exerted an essentially equal bipolar force on this Earth, somewhat distorting its shape, since it was then in the time period of accumulating mass. While it was beginning to form its own structure the binary moon pulled a little bit on it.

The "Victory" of the Occlusions and Our Inheritance from Them

The ancient culture referred to as the Occlusions decided that it would destroy its enemies by destroying itself if necessary. Even today there is that aspect in your society, since you have inherited unresolved problems from the past. One problem is being so angry at another, whether it be a civilization or an individual, that one is willing to destroy oneself in order to destroy the other. This lingers here not only in various criminal acts, but sometimes even in war itself. Sometimes war is considered a great and brave sacrifice; at other times, simply a waste.

That civilization destroyed Earth's binary moon system; thus there was no longer a moon on Earth. Of course, there were catastrophic effects from the weather and the tides and so on. There was a civilization that lived beneath this particular area (and accesses it even today). They took one of the attracting forms of vortex, one of the "feminine" vortexes in an area near Bell Rock, and they grabbed, they borrowed the moon from Mars, pulled it here, and placed it into an orbit before permanent damage was done.

This is an example of some of the not-so-nice things that have occurred here and what is possible to do with a vortex. One might say that if one is deflecting an asteroid that might hit the Earth, even though it is a violent act, it is an act designed to sustain life. Yet if one is destroying something by pushing it into the sun, as was done with the binary moon, one is using the same or similar power to destroy life. You have a polarized society where such things are possible.

The Ancient Underground Sea and Its Pink Dolphins

All right, that was an extreme example of adventure. Now I give you an example that is peaceful and quite wonderful. In the ancient past, associated with the time *before* Atlantis and Lemuria got into big fights, there was a version of dolphins who lived here in a somewhat aquatic area. It was largely an underground sea that had outlets in various areas around here, where you could see from time to time some leftover residual forms of aquatic residues, areas where water was almost lapping upon it. Some areas near Schnebly Hill were associated with this as well as other areas near Bell Rock.

These dolphins lived in an underground sea and would only emerge from time to time to conduct ceremonies to unite the sun and the moon. This may seem strange to you, but dolphins in their essences are highly ceremonial. Anyone who has ever observed any of their rituals will see that they conduct certain acts, certain rollovers and so on in much the same way. These are *spiritual* acts. The dolphin is, of course, a very spiritual person or creature. The dolphins that lived here in that ancient culture were what is referred to loosely by South American cultures as the pink dolphins. They are still connected into some South American regions by underground aquatic seas that are still there.

Montezuma's Well

Could you describe the native community that inhabited the Montezuma's Well area and its relation to Sedona?

This is not a single community. We are referring in this case to the ancient cultures that *created* the well at a time when the water was fresh, pure and drinkable, and to more recent cultures that occupied the areas beneath what could loosely be referred to as the rim. So in terms of the ancient culture, the aquatic sea (referred to as also having elements in Sedona) had an outlet there. If one goes back very far, one can talk about the dolphins. But let us talk about human beings or their prototypes for this discussion tonight.

The Creators of the Sea and the Garden

Those who created the aquatic sea and its various outlets, which run literally through and around Earth to various points of exit and entry, were trained by the Founders. The Founders are those beings who live inside the Earth and assist you in moving through your evolutionary cycles.

Beings trained by the Founders were of the original priest and priestess class that came to be associated with Egypt and other places of ancient culture like Peru and so on. These beings created various functions in this area. In the original early days there was a great garden there, many plants that would provide fruit and vegetables for the people. This was created through the use of accessing seeds and other plant forms through catacomblike tunnels that literally are everywhere underneath the surface of this planet.

Radiation Warfare and Underground Civilization

Things were done *under* the surface rather than *on* the surface at that time due to leftover radiation from a very ancient form of what we could loosely refer to as radiation warfare. I do not not wish to refer necessarily to atomic warfare, because now you use atomic warfare in terms of explosions. The original radiation warfare is more of an implosion designed to evacuate the surface by sucking it into what could loosely be referred to as a temporary black hole. But that is another story.

In any event, the individuals who created that area [Montezuma's Well] were involved in working beneath the planet. Now, some of what they were doing was creating a benign energy that could function to resolve or change radiation. For those of you who may be working on such devices who may read this material some day, be sure to use water in your electromagnetic experiments. Put the instruments under a field of water and they will work much better. They were using these instruments underwater; some of the forms of radiation then were positive radiation, as you understand it. Something that would transform the negative aspects of radiation was done through its emanation through water. Water is the catalyst.

They got things going. They simply used the geological structure that was in place and created what you now know of as Montezuma's Well. Several of the native cultures were even at that time beginning to utilize the rim as a place to settle. You might ask, "But Zoosh! You just talked about this radiation." Yet understand that, as always is the case, whenever there is a form of warfare or struggle there are *always* survivors. Sometimes they are not on the surface; sometimes they are below. In this case there was a remnant civilization that adapted to the radiation and survived on the surface. These people began to use that structure.

The Owls and the Golden Warriors

In time there were other native civilizations that took up this area. Those of you who have perceptions, who can feel, sense, taste, smell, know that there are certain native energies there, can feel the cultures that are still there. I will tell you why. To the native cultures, this is the place of the owl. The owl is seen as a being who assists spirits of the recent dead to find their home and their soul origin. So the owl flies with the spirit of the recent dead.

The civilizations that you will feel there now almost as though there are people there (you will almost feel them pressing against you) are functioning as a form of golden warriors. They are assisting the owls. The owl's spirit energy would appear in human form as a golden warrior. Golden warriors perform the function of finding lost souls. The owl can fly the spirit (in terms of the Native American understanding) to the soul's origin, the place of the Creator, the individual tone or harmonic that is equal to that soul's expression between lives.

Soul Rescuers

Yet what of those that are lost? What of those that die unexpectedly? What of those who have committed suicide? Who helps them, since they have left so many situations unresolved that they need assistance? They need guidance. The warriors of the Golden Dawn will go into the water and, using the ionic energies of the water, will seek that area where all souls reside who have not yet returned to the Creator and are still earthbound due to unresolved dilemmas. You cannot move into the light if there is a huge unresolved emotional conflict. But someone will come and get you; it is not as though you will suffer in some hell-like situation. Someone will come to get you, and the warriors of the Golden Dawn are among those.

Those are the people that live there. They are quite happy and live quite a charming existence. It is not too difficult to see, feel, sense them there.

What dimension are they in?

Warriors from the Ninth Dimension

They are in a dimension that is between the third and the fourth as *you* experience them. They are actually in the ninth dimension. You can experience them when you walk up the stairs and go over to the lookout point and look at the structures to the left, where they are located. When they are prepared to do their work, they essentially descend from the ninth dimension into that position between the third and the fourth dimension, and go into the water. They will go into an area that is "backing up," like a whirling area within that area between the third and the fourth dimension, which is where these souls live, and go inside that parallel Earth to find those souls and bring them to the light of the Creator.

Is the well an entrance to the inner Earth then?

If one can access it on the soul level through spirit, yes, it is. But know this: It is well-guarded; those who have attempted it have found most often their fears heightened. This is how people are kept out. There is no shielding substance, only that of emotion, of sound, of song and physical effort. There are code keys of motion that can be used to pass the first veil into the Earth. I will not give you the keys to pass all the veils. You must be *100%* in alignment with your loving heart energy. All this can be experienced in the area known as Montezuma's Well, and much more.

Do you see when Mother Earth is going into fourth dimension with the new name Terra?

In terms of physical time, you will *feel* it happening right now. It is a process. You will not notice a change because everything is changing equally at the same time. You will not really notice it. But if you imagine everything changing at once, there is no frame of reference to exhibit that change. If you are holding a ruler in your hands and you and your entire world are getting bigger you will not notice that the ruler has become bigger. You are speeding up your consciousness, expanding your reality. Terra is a larger planet than Earth. Did you know that? It contains the same mass but it is larger because it is expanded.

Understand this: Time is difficult to measure because measuring time is a little strange. I will simply say that by the year 2014 you will notice considerable change, but there will still also be some struggle. By that time the new order will be somewhat established.

Can you give us a date when Sedona will be underwater again?

It is beyond a "date." It is a different dimensional aspect. However, it will be several million years in terms of your conscious identification to the space and time ideas. In terms of interdimensional shifts, it would be about as long as [snaps his fingers].

9

Past and Future Civilizations of the Soul's Journey Through Sedona

Bearclaw Through Robert Shapiro
Channeled 3/11/90

Good evening. I am Bearclaw. I am what is described as a Native American mystical man. I lived in the California region several hundred years ago, and through the universal and tribal consciousness I will speak to you now a little bit about the location Sedona, Arizona.

Past Cultures Cyclic, in Motion

There have been many cultures that have roamed through here. I use the word "roam" on purpose, since the idea of indigenous cultures would refer to that which is native to America. While this area itself is surrounded by indigenous cultures —some very ancient, some more recent—this area of Sedona has always been designed to be an area to pass through. The local native populations that lived north and south of here are aware of that. The past civilizations that have occupied this area have always been in motion. That is to say, they have been either fleeting civilizations or they have been civilizations that would move *through* this area, never creating a permanent cycle of life here.

Sometimes in the past there have been certain civilizations that have been brought here, refreshed by the place, and then been released. Know that your purposes for being here are also fleeting. It is desirous that you do not remain here for a lifetime.

The land will not really support you. There is some desire to be here, of course, since the area is magnetic—it draws you to it. Rather than being magnetic in terms of attaching itself to steel or metal, it is magnetic to the rhythm of the soul that lives within you. The area pulls you like a giant ray toward its bosom and nurtures you. Then, like any good mother would, it sends you out into the world refreshed and fulfilled.

The native peoples understand this. I recognize that those who are not so accustomed to Earth ways and Earth rhythms will not necessarily feel the motion of expulsion. Now, I am not telling you to get out. I am just saying that at times when things do not seem to be working, the Sedona Mother wants you to leave—maybe not permanently, maybe for just a day or two—and go out and spread the word of Sedona elsewhere. This does not mean promoting Sedona, but spreading the word of the heart and the knowledge of the heart and the energy of the heart.

Emotional Stimulation

This area primarily stimulates emotions and emotional nurturance. Many of you may have noticed that the experience of the emotional body here is very powerful and almost impossible to avoid. You will have unexpected flare-ups of emotion, and at other times you seem more at peace with the world than in any other place. The area is genuinely magnetic in that way. In your physical bodies there are minerals drawn that act as a function of a magnetic opposite polarity and allow you to be drawn here. That is what is going on on your level. That is how we see it.

Future civilizations that will occur here will again be cyclic in origin. People will come, people will go. The future of this place is primarily that of an artistic colony. In the past it has been primarily spiritual in nature, ancient in its spirituality. That spirit and art are connected is a given. Art expressed as spirit is also a given. Many of you have noticed that the rock formations seem to be emerging as a form of sculpture. There is controversy about whether it is ancient sculpture that is wearing away, or whether perhaps it is something that seems to be emerging from the rock itself as if by divine order.

In a sense, these are really *future relics*. Imagine for a moment the idea of a thought as it forms in your head. Sometimes there is inspiration, and then you build greatly upon that inspiration and form a large body of information or ideas associated with that one original thought. In a sense it is like that. You have a large body of artwork, spiritual artwork, that will fully surround this area in many ways in the distant future. Now, what is occurring is as though the thought, the inspiration, and the artwork is emerging under its inspired energy for the future.

Many times inspiration requires interaction between the human element and the stone in order to bring that artwork out. Any good sculptor knows that the stone is not carved *into* something, but that the stone is removed to reveal the form that lies within. Thus it is happening here that forms are revealing themselves ever so slightly, so that sculptors in the future can very reverentially carve them into the shapes in which they seem to be trying to express.

The Overseeing Kachina Energies

Understand that many different kachina energies will oversee this place. Many of these are representations of the elements. The elements in this case are the sun, the wind, the moon, the light, the stars, and so on. Some kachinas will draw you here like nurturing mothers; others will embrace you and assist you to do what you came here to do. Others, the strong papas, will give you the strength to believe in your own abilities, and send you out, if only on a short trip, to bring to others the gifts you uniquely have to offer. Sedona draws you like a magnet and then hurls you out into the world after it has changed you. This is what this place is for. This has *always* been what it was for.

Know that the native peoples can see the kachina energies on many of the rock formations, most of them dancing on the top. A kachina, in order to fulfill its primary purpose, *must be in motion* and can never be truly captured in its actual form and function unless it is moving. You might see art forms, small sculptures or even large versions in dance, and yet the real image of the kachina can never be captured unless the individual is in motion. Know that these kachinas protect and assist you. They are designed to bring forth the best in you.

Know also this: kachina energy is not complacent. Even the feminine versions, the gentle and nurturing versions, are not complacent. They are demanding energies. They will demand the very best from you and you'll not be able to resist. If you stay here you must achieve the highest level of your goal that you can at this time in this place. It will be demanded of you. Otherwise you will feel a constant emotion that gnaws away at you. That emotion will be rejection.

For those of you that might feel rejected from time to time, know it is only this. It is not that the kachinas are rejecting you, but that you are rejecting what they have to offer. Any emotion or desire that you have can be supported by any of the kachina energies here—there is even a kachina that will support conflict, for sometimes in conflict there is great growth possible. Sometimes in sacrifice there is growth. Sometimes in struggle there is growth, because there is always the possibility of conquering fears and doubts and moving into that portion of your life that is the most uplifting.

Know this: Sedona supports you ever from the past, the future, and the present to become the best that you can be. Know this, understand it, and allow it to exist.

I'd like to ask about the idea of Sedona being a place where people pass through. I'm certainly aware of that. Yet I've gotten to know a lot of people who have lived here for 10, 20, 30 years.

I do not rule out the fact that people might stay indefinitely. I do say that to get the very best out of this place, one might not necessarily have to live here. You understand that many, many people need to come here in order to be refreshed and sustained, as one might go to a water hole in the middle of the desert. You will be refreshed, sustained and then you go on. You don't stay there. Some people do; some will stay and tend the water hole, or build a structure to enjoy the water. Yet many pass through. I am not ruling out those who stay, but I am suggesting that even those who have been here for 20 or 30 years consider taking their knowledge, information and wisdom and spreading it about wherever they go—whether it be through thought, deed, action, the written word, or any other means of communication.

Past Native Ceremonies

Could you describe the nature of any ceremonies that the native peoples used?

You have already begun to do medicine wheels, so I will skip over that. Sweat lodge ceremonies were also involved here. I will suggest what some of the mystical men and women of the time did. I will use Boynton Canyon as an example, since in its deepest portion—that which is flush up against the rock, where the rock meets the land—there were prayers done to stimulate growth of plants and trees that would support the physical human being.

To begin with, there were motions made that were designed to emulate that of growing things. When things grow, they come out of the ground in forms and shapes of motion that could only be described as dance. These unfolding types of dances were done to encourage the Earth to bring forth food and sustenance for the people who lived and passed through this area.

Those of you who wish to change some structures here, to encourage some elements of edible wild plants and to practice in the way of the shaman can begin by imagining what it is like for a plant to come out of the ground and unfold to provide food and sustenance for all that is around it.

It is, in many senses, a great gift; yet at the same time it is a sacrifice. Sacrificing one's life to sustain another is admired by many human beings. You may make a small sacrifice of your time and energy by going out and doing these dances according to how you might imagine them to be. I am not saying you *must*, but those of you would like to, that is a way. It is something you can do to support the land and the populations that pass through.

50 Civilizations Ago

Someone who has been here for a long time came before a lama, who said he had been here 50 civilizations ago in Sedona. I would like to know if that would be in millions of years ago? What would be 50 civilizations ago?

That was in the time when there was a continental shelf connecting the northern area of China to the northern area of what is now referred to as Canada/Alaska. At that time the civilizations from those two continents freely passed amongst the continents, so there was a greater understanding of world knowledge. Sophisticated cultures abounded, since there was a constant exchange of information. It is less necessary to give you a time, but I would say, roughly (if you must have one), a million to a million and a half years ago. That continental shelf has now disappeared beneath the sea so that you could experience power struggles.

Understand that in order for resolution to take place, there must be sufficient conflict for people to *seek* resolution. If enough people seek resolution, they will find it.

Is there a kachina energy for each vortex?

Vortexes and Their Associated Kachinas

The kachinas are somewhat divided, associated with the elements. The vortices are an emotion; they move. Though one area might seem to exist as a specific type of vortex, these energies are in constant motion. I will give you a few examples.

The **kachina for rain** is located in the area referred to as **Eagle Rock.** That is out toward Boynton Canyon. This eagle energy will divine what is needed for any given place and time and provide that through its vision. It is as though an eagle spirit is entrapped in the rock in such a way that it always is attempting to see what is beyond, what is coming, and what is needed. We perceive that that type of energy will bring to this land what is needed.

In terms of the kachina associated with the **Airport Vortex,** it is naturally the **kachina of flight,** of imagination—that is to say, of stimulating imaginative possibilities for difficult problems. If you have a problem that you cannot solve, sometimes embracing and enveloping yourself in the energy of the kachina of imagination will assist you.

As for **Bell Rock**, that is the **kachina of hope and spirit**. It allows you to move through many possibilities that seem to drag you down. For those of you with afflictions or even addictions, you can be stimulated towards greater strength by Bell Rock.

I am not pointing and saying that these are healing grounds and so bring all your sick, injured and disabled. I am suggesting that if there is some aspect of your consciousness that is addicted or sorry for itself, Bell Rock can shake that loose and assist you to move from those positions.

Is there a kachina for Cathedral Rock?

This is the **kachina of wisdom** on the side that faces the area known as the Village of Oak Creek. On the side that faces the other direction, it is the **kachina of conflict**. Understand that there are not normally two kachinas. But since wisdom will sometimes get you through conflict, and since conflict will sometimes stimulate wisdom, it is believed that these two are two sides of the same idea.

What is the kachina for Courthouse?

This is the **kachina for lightning**, which has to do with action, or immediacy. Those of you who feel slowness or delays might go out to this area, perform a dance, give a prayer, and ask for ideas to stimulate you toward actions to resolve that which is delayed. The reason for dance and motion has less to do with ritual than with presenting yourself to the Great Spirit as a physical being who interacts in the physical world. As you present yourself to the Earth spirit, then you allow yourself to ask for what you want in sign language. Perhaps you feel delayed; things are moving too slowly. So you ask for motion, for things to be speeded up. You do this in performance, because all human beings are reaching for grace. When you desire grace, you must attempt as much gracefulness as you know how. Use your imagination. You do not have to be beautiful

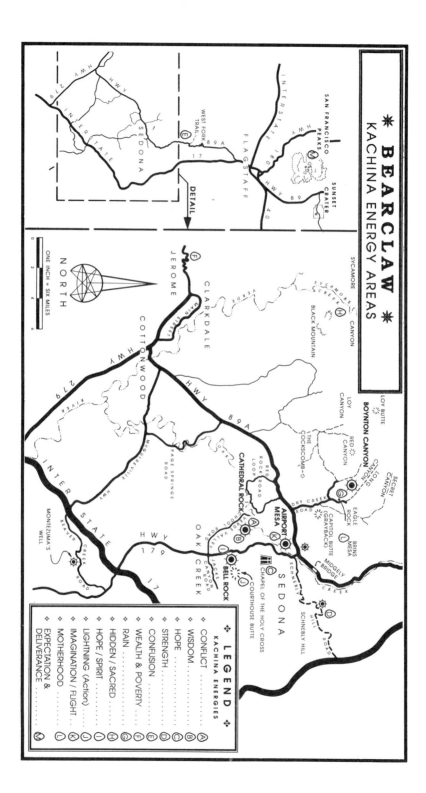

with the dance, but let the dance express what you want.

I think Eagle Rock is the same thing as Coffee Pot. Can you mention the kachinas?

To my understanding, Eagle Rock would be referred to as another area. It is not Coffee Pot, as you call it, though there are those that refer to it as such.

My favorite place to walk is on the Jordan Road trail at least as far as the shooting range, and then to Brim's Mesa. I'd like to know about the energy there.

Brim's Mesa is the **kachina of motherhood**, a female kachina. It is a nurturing area, although the activities around the area are not always supportive of what would be appear to be nurturance.

What about the San Francisco Peaks and West Fork?

The **San Francisco Peaks** kachina is of **expectation and deliverance**. Recognize again that you have two sides to the same idea. Expectation very often keeps things away, and yet deliverance provides. You must ask out loud for what you want. Be as physical in your asking as you can so that it is delivered to you physically. If you think about what you want, it may be delivered in thought, fantasy, or imagination, but that is all. This is why native peoples dance, because they want things to be delivered to them in physical fact.

As for **West Fork**, the energy associated with that might be **confusion**. Now, I do not mean that you should stay away from the area, but it *is* an area in which you might feel pulled in many different directions at once. If you are seeking to be stimulated out of a sense of dullness, you might go there and be stimulated perhaps too much, because within confusion is its opposite, **stimulation**. Thus you might feel very stimulated, but you could also feel very scattered.

What about Sycamore Canyon? the Chapel? Schnebly Hill?

In terms of kachina energy, **Sycamore Canyon** is the energy of the **hidden and most sacred**. This kachina may not stay there for much longer, since the hidden has almost totally been found. To some extent, that which has been found has been misused. This kachina may relocate. I will not say where, but it will be near the Superstition Mountains, which is an area that is protected beyond that which the human being can encroach.

The **Chapel** is an area that is the **kachina of hope.**

Schnebly Hill is the **kachina of strength.** Those who mount the kachina of strength by mounting the hill that represents it will feel the value of their physical reality. It is designed to stimulate an interest in physical reality and is, of course, located high up at the very top so that one can see the varieties of physical reality. The next canyon after that [**Oak Creek Canyon**] is designed to stimulate an **appreciation for Mother Earth.** This is what strength will often do, since strength's true gift is safety. When one feels safe on Mother Earth, there is almost nothing that you cannot do.

Could you tell us about the vortex in Jerome, Arizona?

I will not speak of vortexes but of kachinas. The kachina for the area of **Jerome** (located at the very uppermost portion of the most recent digging operation) is the **kachina of wealth and poverty.** It has many faces, wealth and poverty, and one side of the kachina is filled with furs and golden droplets in the form of jewelry. The other side is in rags. Yet this kachina is the proudest of all, since it represents a form of desire and equally represents a form of acceptance. This kachina is perhaps the most wise.

Different Vortexes for Different Healing Levels

If four people came to Sedona and each of them needed healing on a different level—physical, mental, emotional and spiritual—where would you ask each of them to go?

Bell Rock (physical), Boynton Canyon (mental), Airport (emotional), Schnebly Hill (spiritual). Even though Schnebly Hill is not considered to be a vortex, strength and safety are almost more necessary now than the spiritual that will sustain you.

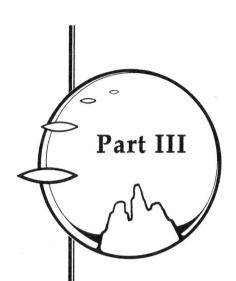

Part III

INTERDIMENSIONAL
ADVENTURES

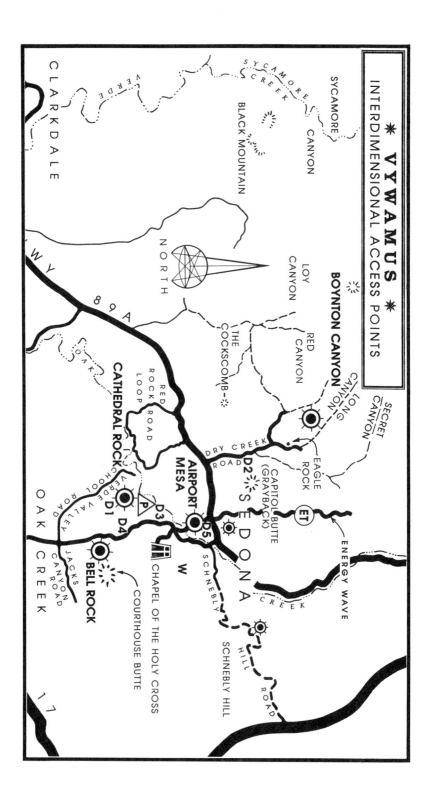

10

Dimensional Openings in Sedona

Vywamus Through Janet McClure
Channeled 2/19/90

I have indicated a thick wavy line going through both the Airport Vortex and the Chapel of the Holy Cross and on out to Soldier's Pass Road. It continues, of course; it doesn't end where I've quit drawing it. This is a dimensional switching. The fifth, fourth, and third dimensions are joined through the second, which is really a corridor of connecting energy. So there is a tremendous surge of energy in this area. One doesn't always feel it right there, but if you could literally ride it from one end to the other, it would be quite a ride indeed! It crests at the Chapel of the Holy Cross and then, in a sense, goes down to the area of Soldier's Pass Road.

There is a response to what the dimensions mean by traveling this energy. You can travel it physically, but you can also travel it in your visualizations or meditations. That should put you in touch with flow, the magnification of your creativity, and understanding purpose in structure. If you would include in your Sedona trip visualizations of flowing this energy corridor, it is like skiing over an energy flow that opens for you a broader view and experience within several dimensions simultaneously. You are, of course, multidimensional, but many of you don't recognize it. This energy wave puts it all together for you and shows you how to use this energy in an integrated manner.

If you consider yourself to be intuitive or to have a good imagination, I think you will very much enjoy "skiing" through this dimensional joining point.

Mapping Sedona

The points I have marked **D** on the map have the inter-dimensional effect of an entry or **doorway** to other dimensions. It is easy to get lost in such an entryway. I would suggest that you not try to use one unless you are very sure how to do so. Some of you have gone into such doorways only to find it was much easier to go in than get out. In fact, some of you never *did* figure your way out of them.

I have entered on the map several dimensional entry points. I am being purposefully just a little bit vague, because in order to find them exactly you need to be ready for it. There are five interdimensional doorways here used by those of us who know how to use them and by those from other planets.

My definition of a **window** (**W** on the map) would be the part of Sedona that looks out over a corresponding or twin universe, another universe quite similar in nature. It is not meant that one go there, but an opening is created by knowing where it is. It can be a mirror to those who know its location and can use the potential from that universe. When you open up a window, you let in, hopefully, a fresh breeze, a fresh new way of looking at and using the creativity stored there. In a meditation you may open a window to this universe, let it into your life and let it refresh your life. It will work. It may do some deep cleansing for you also, but it certainly will bring in the new perspectives you have been seeking.

I have placed a **P** within a triangle on the map to indicate a **portal**. There are many ways of looking at each of these terms; every spiritual teacher you ask will talk about them a little differently. But to me a portal is a point that can, through its energy, help you to access another level, another opportunity, another point of view. You use a window differently; you simply look out at another universe or bring a little of it to you. A portal, however, actually moves your energy *into* that other area—although in the broadest sense you still remain here. It broadens the application of your energy, letting it go beyond just one point of view by bringing in other points of view.

One such point is a portal. If you learn to use several portals, then you are bringing opportunities from several points into this particular point (your present perspective) by taking your energy there and then using the energy grid system to move that experience and what you've learned back to this point. So there is an actual energy interaction when you use a portal, although with a window there is not.

An Underground ET Base

In the area where I've put ET in a circle there is a deep underground base. Spaceships fly in and out there; the reason I can label it so clearly is that it is very well protected. Until you are ready you are not going to find it. You could go right to it, and it would not be there for you. When you are ready spiritually, you will get in touch with it, because many of the beings who are connected with this underground area are the ones you are working with in your purposes on the inner planes. They live in the same neighborhood, except their base is very deep underground. That is my only comment now.

Meditating at Vortexes

I feel that doing certain meditations at the energy points is the key for empowering yourself through the Sedona energies. Choose a power point: Bell Rock, Boynton Canyon or any other —not only the main ones (although you will want to start with them) but any developing energy point in the area that you can help build through your association with it. Use your knowingness to select the points—the major ones and the location *within* the major ones, as well as the minor points you are helping to develop through building them through your energy structure.

Remember that you are a creator, and the energies of Sedona can be built through the creator part of you. You are also a co-creator and as such can help stabilize the energies of others through your willingness to be a part of these energy points. Choose one and go to it. Become quiet and allow the elementals and the angelic presences within that vortex to work out your association with the vortex. You don't have to do anything, as the connections are being made for you. Certainly there needs to be an openness, a willingness. Beyond that, just being there for a few moments quietly begins the process.

Connecting with Angels and Elementals

The experience will vary for you at the different energy points. It will also be different for you at different times. It will be different for you in that you have unique abilities that are not the same as everyone else's. But what it will be for *all* of you is a connection and a point of progressing your understanding of *what power really means* on the Earth. Because I am what is known as a spiritual psychiatrist, I can say to you that power is an interesting area for all of you. Some of you have had experiences that cause you to feel that power is something to run away from. Power was misused either by you or by others, and you felt the effect of that misuse. Now you can build up your trust in the area of accepting your power by meditating and connecting with the angelic and elemental presences within the vortexes.

If you are seeking to understand a relationship more clearly, bring that relationship into the vortex. You can bring the physical person with you or, if that is not possible, bring your memories and your connection to that person into the vortexes and meditate on it. It takes a little time, usually several times in one vortex, before you can be as connected to it as you would like. My suggestion would be to go to one several times before you go on to another. I know some of you will go from one to the other. But if you are seeking to aid the Earth and you have time enough, it can be helpful to go to one vortex several times and then to another several times so that you build your energy connection to that particular power point.

Understanding Soul's Purpose

If you are seeking to understand your soul's purpose more clearly, if you are seeking to surrender to the Plan more clearly and to understand what this means, then meditation within such a power point will assist you. However, it may not assist you in the way you anticipate. It may simply point up some resistances, which must then be cleared out. But it *will* process you in the areas where you ask for help. Remember, while you are in the power points (if you wish), to ask the Earth to use your energies where she needs them the most. It may be that through a powerful projection from Sedona to the Middle East, your energies can make a difference there.

Sedona magnifies your ability to learn through energy. It increases it ten times and then ten times more and ten times still further. The longer you are here, the more sensitive you become to the use of energy. Certainly, you can get completely insensitive, but if you allow your sensitivity to keep increasing, it will. It will keep growing and help you align into a clearer type of life and fulfillment of your soul's purpose.

There are critical points on the Earth, and the energies of Sedona can help clear the use of all parts of the Earth. In order to create a new age that is a unified, integrative and responsive vortex of overall consideration for others, take into consideration all of the strengths that you and everyone else has, stir them together to bring that powerful new age where everyone fulfills his or her purpose and enjoys living upon a peaceful Earth.

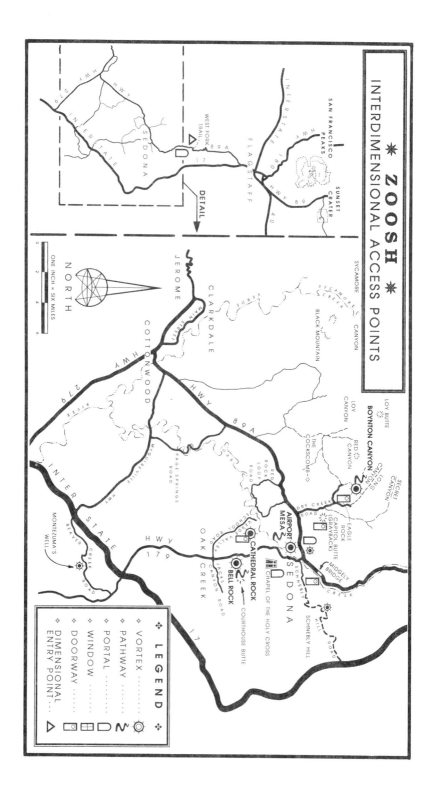

11

Doorways, Pathways, Portals and Caves

Zoosh Through Robert Shapiro
Channeled 9/10/89

L et us first define our terms. A **doorway** would be an entrance. It would feel as if something had actually slid back to open up a passageway for you. A **portal** might conveniently be something that could free-float in space or be a tunnel to take you to some other place. A pathway, however, is a little different. A **pathway** would require something of you. It would require more than being in spiritual balance and alignment. It might require that you perform certain motions. These motions might be like the unlocking of a safe. These motions are used in prescribed ways. You could take that pathway not only to elsewhere, but also to power. So let us begin with pathways.

Pathways: Some Locations
The new forms of energy and focus these days will have much more to do with motion than with thought. Some motions that will help you create your own Arthur Murray dance step might (in order to unlock many keys for yourself) be stimulated by the code keys of language and symbols. I'd attempt to translate it directly, but sometimes those translations are involved less with a specific intellectual meaning than with a meaning triggered by the unlocking of a conscious or unconscious code key, which is in turn triggered by motion. Consider that.

In pathways to other dimensions, you would have to move in certain ways. To some extent, all of the thought in the world will not prepare you for this, because it cannot be done with precision. It cannot work by doing it precisely the same way every time. So it will have to be achieved through spontaneous action designed to recreate the physical and emotional energy in that region.

There are several pathways in Sedona. Pathways are always the keys to power, because they will require something of you. So we will talk about the keys first, since you are all interested in that.

There are three well-defined pathways here. One leads to the past; one leads to the future. The third leads to an expanded version of the present, which would allow you to see the overlays of conscious reality that exist in this now dimension and experience it as a multidimensional version of yourself while at the same time being aware of those multidimensional experiences.

One might conceive of this as vertical time. Now, there are different dimensions, different pulses that exist in this space right now as I speak. And as such, there are different versions of many of you in many of these places. As a result, if you could be consciously aware and process both thoughtfully and energetically all that is going on—all of those versions of you and all of the nows that exist in this time moment at this present—you would perhaps have a great deal more of you present to deal with your world.

This cannot be unlocked without a motion. Much of the world's martial arts are dances of homage to these motions, though they might be used for other purposes. Perhaps the best example would be Tai Chi, though it has become more of a discipline and less of a creative expression of motion.

Bell Rock is the place for the pathway to the expanded reality that I am discussing. I will, of course, not give you the exact place, because you must be sensitized to energy. It is conceivable that those of you who are involved in motion practice as well as spiritual alignment could find it. Now, however, you might wish to find it in order to escape, and that is not the program. Within 20 years it will be found, but it is not possible that its access be controlled. That is to say, even now people will step from elsewhere through that doorway, but mostly it is a pathway to consciousness expansion.

Feel around for where it might be. But do your practice of motion elsewhere, lest you unlock the combination unexpectedly. You will know you are close to doing that if you suddenly feel as if you hear things, feel things, and all your senses are stimulated. It is not like feeling dizzy. You *might* feel dizzy at a portal, but it is not that. You will suddenly have your senses greatly expanded: You will hear a bird chirping on the other side of the valley. You will hear leaves moving in a tree a thousand yards away. You will hear grains of sands knocking against each other as they blow across the face of Bell Rock. You will feel the undulations of the breeze moving across your body as you've never felt it before. In other words, it will be a heightened experience of sensuality.

There is a pathway associated with **Boynton Canyon**—again I am being vague, but it is to protect you somewhat from stumbling in. The pathway in Boynton Canyon is to the past. Now, recognize that these are time doors, one might say, and the pathway will be unlocked by what you do. As a result, it is unlikely that these types of pathways will be stumbled into. (Portals, now *that* is something different!)

Airport Vortex is a pathway to the future. People will sometimes tell you experiences they have had there. The motions involved in that pathway to the future are very minuscule. It is possible to make certain common motions and gestures that will sufficiently open into the future for you to have what could be loosely referred to as an overlay experience. In that case, you would feel yourself present here, but *there* as well.

Moving Doorways

Doorways do not remain where they are. Pathways will usually remain somewhat, as they are in a localized area. This is really for your protection, because it is conceivable that people using forms of martial arts might accidentally step through a doorway unexpectedly. So doorways move around and have a form of consciousness in their own right. Yet those that access other worlds as well as other dimensions might remain where they are if they are not on a trail or a road. Sometimes they will be formed on the rock faces, but not usually where climbers will be, simply because it wouldn't do at all to have them reach for a handhold and go into the rock! That would be alarming, to say the least.

Feeling the Portals

Portals will perhaps be most noticeable by their localized feeling. You can walk through a portal and have a funny feeling in your chest. You might suddenly feel a little odd, a little strange. Perhaps you might completely relax, or suddenly feel kind of wiggly. You might also feel dizzy if the portal is big enough to encapsulate you or if the energy is very pronounced.

Imagine, if you would, the idea of a tube, for portals are essentially round. For example, there is a portal right smack in the middle of your downtown tourist area in a store! It comes and goes, as it were, somewhat whimsically. But it is there. If you were standing there at the right time, it wouldn't make any difference what motions you were making—you could step through, and this is how you would experience it: Even though it would not be an accident, you would suddenly have a flash of some other reality. I am not comparing this directly to inspiration, which might give you a flash, but portals are associated with *deja vu* experiences. They are the receiving end of a dream, a reality, or a future laid out for you. When you meet that future on the map of your life, you will meet it at a portal.

Will you comment on the statuelike rock at Chapel of the Holy Cross that appears to be the Madonna and child?

A Time Portal

That particular location has a portal to that specific time; it comes and goes. It can be seen in certain situations as a gold circle. Sometimes it can be felt as heat. This is not a rule of portals as you understand them, but it *is* the case of that particular portal. That portal will, if you choose, reveal to you in meditations, thoughts, or even physical reality the time of the Madonna and Child.

There are statuelike rocks right in town under Capital Butte that look like a Lemurian temple. Is there a portal there? Would that connect one to the Lemurian times?

Doorway to a Distant System

There is a doorway. Often doorways are here. There are other aspects of doorways. Sometimes there are physical things that must be done, though not exactly like moving a rock and having a door swing open. Doorways are like energy fields that you feel, and you put your hand forward in certain ways, touching certain aspects of that rock in a certain sequence or perhaps with a certain energy expelled from your hand. It is going to protect itself; it will open up only if no one is looking at you at that moment—because, obviously, if you are standing in front of a crowd of people and you step through a doorway, that is going to make the news! So in order to protect these doorways, it will have to be done as discreetly as possible, for doorways allow a great deal of access from other sides.

The doorway referred to in the question, though it appears to be Lemurian (and people have interpreted it as that), actually goes to another world entirely. It goes to a distant galaxy [star system] from which some of these Lemurian ideas were sourced. Again, the idea of Lemuria has to do with dance and motion. It is coming from several planets in the constellation Orion that are known for music, song, light, sound and synchronized variations of these.

These worlds will receive not only your feelings, thoughts, interpretations and communication beyond what you understand intellectually, but they will respond by *sending individuals*. Sometimes they will send energies. For those of you who have taken photographs around these areas, you may see things on the photographs that seem to emanate from rocks and appear to be spirit energies. At that moment, in that particular rock, it almost always would be an emanation of an energy personality through a portal or a doorway from some other source allowing itself to be seen.

These energy beings coming in from those sources will respond largely to your needs. Perhaps it is a spoken need through prayer, for example. Or perhaps it is an unspoken subconscious need that will express itself as an emotion that many, many people will feel at the same time. It is possible for these energy beings to come and radiate through these doorways various energies that will unlock or stimulate changes in all of you so that those emotions can be expressed and the lessons fulfilled and understood. It is as though you are sending a message, you see. It is true that you can step through these doorways in certain circumstances as indicated, but the true purpose is for others to step through for *you*.

If you go through the door harmonically, how do you get back?

Ah, there's the rub. Maybe you don't. This is an important question that has been asked. If you go through the doorway, how do you get back? Very simply, maybe you don't. This is the responsibility. Like the hobby of exploring caves, it is a rather dangerous adventure, and yet very rewarding, fulfilling, fun and so on. There is at least a 50/50 chance that you will get back, perhaps considerably better if you are prepared. Yet in this case the chances of getting back are perhaps one-half of one percent. Not a good bet. So understand this: If you are going to experiment with this, make sure your life is in order first!

People have mentioned some activity in Long Canyon and Secret Canyon. They have taken photographs and have seen some sort of astral machines out there. Can you comment on that?

Negative-ET Underground Base

It is, as you know, your function on this world you are living in to be somewhat of a psychodramatic clearing house for not only yourselves as souls to resolve problems you have been unable to resolve elsewhere, but for whole societies within your galaxy that have been unable to resolve certain sticky issues. This planet, this society and this race were created to act as a clearing house for those difficult-to-resolve problems.

Understand that you are connected to all of these places as well as points in time where you have had problems on the soul level. On previous occasions I've stated that there are certain areas and certain groups who are negatively oriented, such as the little planet in Sirius. Those individuals have a doorway here. Do not be alarmed. I will simply say that they have an underground base. One of their facilities has become known to be in the Nevada area through various forms of publicity. The base stretches out now into portions of Utah, even a little in Texas, northern Arizona, northern New Mexico; not too much in Colorado yet, and reaching for California—all underground.

Do not be overly concerned; they are doing what they feel they can do. Since you are attached to these people, that attachment is designed for the enlightenment of you both. That is to say, they have been unable to resolve their own experience of negative energy by themselves, but they can relate to you somewhat because you experience some negative energy, perhaps more than other planets in your galaxy. As a result, it is the only way for them to pass into the third dimension. You are going to the fourth dimension and they must pass into the third dimension.

As you move from this planet onto the fourth-dimensional aspect of this planet, they will inherit its third-dimensional aspect. They do not know this. I give this to you as background material because there is a place in that specific area that is a portal they can sometimes access. However, even though your government is not exactly aware of this, those beings cannot access it to exit into your society and come up into your world. These people, of course, live elsewhere, but they are utilizing this underground base. Although they cannot come up into your world, they can take some things in. I am not saying to stay out of there "because the big bad wolf is going to get you."

Where is the base?

Black Helicopters

It is near Boynton Canyon. They will suck energy in from there in the hope of understanding through analysis of energies what they can do to "win," from their point of view. I do not want to digress greatly about who they are. That material is available. Certain earth vehicles [black helicopters] that have been seen in the area are designed more to protect *you* than they are designed to look threatening—all right, sometimes they look threatening. But you must ask yourself this, my friends: if the people flying around in these vehicles wanted to remain anonymous, wouldn't they look like regular vehicles?

There has been some attempt to make a show of their presence not only to create an enigma and to stimulate your curiosity (because that is involved in the plan), but also to keep you away. Do not always assume that your government has some conspiratorial design. Sometimes they will create something that looks a little bit scary to keep people away.

Government's Protective ELF Pulses

I will also say (without revealing any great big secrets) that your government has established a radionic device underground in that particular area that can radiate a certain pulse along the extra-low-frequency range, which may create a feeling of discomfort but not make you sick. It will cause you to *want* to stay away. It is like a burglar alarm; in a sense, you are the burglar. It is a benign device to keep you out. Do not assume that your government is just out to get you. They are, very often, unsung heroes. I am not campaigning here, but I am suggesting that there is something going on out there such that it would be better if you didn't go there. There will be, in time, revelations by official authorities. They may not necessarily tell it to you as it is, but they will tell you *some* of what they know. Even so, it will sound pretty sensational, and it has been a struggle for them to keep it secret. That is the negative portal.

Is there something underground at the resort near Boynton Canyon?

Boynton's Underground Crystal Antenna

There is a resonant energy wave. As it turns out, under that area it is enchanted, literally! Under that area there are crystal streams, so it is like the ultimate antenna. Anything that is going on energetically nearby may be affected or amplified. Imagine, if you can, for example, a spider web in all of its beauty. Underneath this enchanted area there is a spider web of crystal veins that runs deep, creating a "dish antenna," to use an analogy. It can both radiate and receive, and its intended purpose was for geomancy as well as geography and geology. However, it is not greatly defeated by having the structures [the resort] there.

I will simply say that the area is not bewitched, but it *is* enchanted, in the sense that it is possible, due to the crystal veins, to experience totally different realities there. You can take a walk in that area and feel as though you are stepping through one doorway after another while you are remaining in this doorway. So one might say it is like a petri dish for life. If used to its highest purpose, it would perhaps be used by the spiritualists and healers and religious leaders of your planet. Perhaps in time it will be used that way. Yet it must be used carefully and with reverence, for that is its purpose. Sometimes, if there is some negative energy nearby, it can resonate like a tuning fork might resonate to a created tone, but is not in its own right producing that tone. In time, that resonance is likely to be toned down due to the area's building a force of energy that will, we shall say, balance that negative resonance.

All that the negative individuals need to become a little more positive is actually coded into that area. Much of the crystal web is etheric, so one might have occasional feelings of what could be misinterpreted as ghost energy. That is to say, you could go for a walk there, be in clear space, and yet walk through something that would feel latticelike, or strangely like a slightly physical energy. This is in case the area is ever attacked or mined, one might say. There is a sufficient etheric crystal web in place to do the job, but it would be better not to dig around there too much.

Could you comment on Eagle Rock and the energy there?

A Doorway to Possibilities

Thank you. The energy there has to do with a doorway to possibilities. In a sense, it is a doorway to imagination, an increased level of imagination. It must be used very carefully, of course, because it is conceivable that one might have imaginings that are not always pleasant. But if you can utilize and focus all of your attention on something you imagine to be very pleasant, you could have in that particular area the pinpoints on the chart seeded into you that will help to attract you to that experience. So here you are talking about something that is more than an energetic doorway or even a portal. It changes, rather than being something that is specifically designed to take you to another world.

Zoosh, is there an entrance into the inner Earth in West Fork?

West Fork's Interdimensional/Inner Earth Entrance

There is an interdimensional entrance in that general area. It is possible to not only go inside the earth in this dimension, but once inside the earth, pass into other dimensions. There have already been three individuals who have gone inside on the physical level. Only one person has actually stepped in all the way. He came back to try and figure out what happened. Understand that without an expanded consciousness, doing these things could literally drive a person insane. It would be as though you walked into the Library of Congress, for example, and expected to receive and process all of that information at once.

There is a way into that area. The gestures required to go into other worlds are very simple; sometimes you will make a very innocent gesture, like placing the hand on the face. That innocent gesture may be a common, ordinary one that could activate a particular passage—and that would never do. So I will simply say that yes, it is there, and it goes beyond your wildest dreams.

Is there a passageway that works with all kinds of elementals?

You don't need to go there to do that! And I would not recommend that you do that. Because if you went there and could find your way back (which would be a real trick), you would not look like you look now. Chances are you would have, as the folk like to say, a pretty wild-eyed look. You might not be able to conduct a normal life after that!

Is this the Rip Van Winkle effect you are talking about?

When Rip woke up, he looked well-rested! It would be as if you were in a world you didn't understand. You could come back to that point, but you could never put it back the way it was. Once that is exposed, it remains exposed.

There are people even now in mental institutions who have gone beyond, but have not been able to process it. Because, you understand, we are talking about a world that is beyond any correlation to anything that you know now. There is not a single model of thought available to you enabling you to say, "Oh, so that's what it was!"—nothing! And you would be surrounded with millions of inputs like that. It would not be conceivable to stay encapsulated in your physical body or even in your personality. If you got back, you would not say, "Oh well, life goes on." I do not recommend it as an experience.

You were speaking earlier of this heightened awareness. Does going through a portal like that release vibrations that would be like experiencing LSD?

That is a wonderful analogy. It would do what lysergic acid does, but that is very tiny compared to *this* experience. I do not recommend it along the pathway to growth, but the reason it exists is largely for other things to come *out* into your world. It is designed to be an exit. Even though someone may stand at the other side and say, "Oh no—exit, not entrance!" you can always go in the exit, though you might not like what you find when you get there.

Zoosh, do you have any comments on Carlos Castaneda and the **Tales of Power,** *which is a complete set of guidebooks to do just what you are talking about?*

Castaneda's How-To Books

I will not criticize; I will simply say that the real message of those books is not so much getting there (going through the dimensions); it is what you must do to get to the point where you can *then* go through the dimensions. When you are at the point of having done all of these things, it is very unlikely that you will want to leave. Think about it.

If you were to leave before the fulfillment of your purpose on this planet in this time now, what is the real value? Why do you think that so many native cultures (especially in the Southwest) have traditions among their mystical men and women that are designed to help them to transform themselves into animals and understand other realities while on Earth? It is so they can come back and give their people other ways of living on this planet as it is now. But why go to other places that may not necessarily relate directly to this planet? My comment on those books is that they are of complete value since they are more about *"how* I got there," rather than "there" itself.

Experiencing Aspects of Inner Earth

Are there any aspects of the civilization in the inner Earth that we can participate with physically here in Sedona?

In a sense. If you can do some of this spontaneous dance movement, you can begin. Much of what goes on in inner Earth is indicated as the flow of life. Notice that it is not stated as the *thought* of life, but the *flow,* because your life physically as well as life everywhere is in motion on a microcosmic level. Your physicists can prove that. Life is in motion. All of these objects are actually in motion right now, certainly on the atomic level.

So understand that you can begin to have moments of inspired motion. Don't stand there and wait for inspiration to come in; begin to move. You can begin that experience just sitting around the house—if you feel awkward or funny making motions while you are talking, then you can always move around or rock. I'll have to tell you that if motion was hard to do, rocking chairs wouldn't be too popular! People sit in them and enjoy it. It is a wonderful feeling. It feels kind of reassuring.

I understand that your world sometimes causes you to feel that if you don't move, you'll be safe. Certainly in some extreme situations of survival, not moving might be of value. But there are other situations of survival where moving is of real value.

So begin to move around more. In the inner Earth people do not walk anywhere, even if they are embodied. They *dance*. There is a fluidity of motion that you might refer to as grace, such as in ballet. Notice the way ballet dancers walk. They have supreme confidence in their physical self, and if they felt permission they might do some of these motions. I cannot stress it too strongly.

What about Cathedral Rock? Is there a doorway or portal there?

Cathedral Rock, Portal to a Being State

There is a portal to a state of being. That's the closest way to describe it. It is to a state of being of alter ego. This could be conceived of as both positive and negative. Many years ago, before your civilization was really well established, there was a lot of violence in that area. That is because if you are not conscious or cognizant of the energies of this region, it is possible for the negative thoughts you never acted on to be stimulated, as well as your positive thoughts.

It is like an anticipated event or a wishing well where wishes come true. Recognize that one need not even consider stepping through a doorway to alter ego there. The energy is *present*. Looking at it at its most delightful, for example, it might be a good place to propose to someone if you've been kind of shy about bringing it up! It is what you have seen in your mind's eye as your idealized proposal and its graceful acceptance by the other. It might have a better chance of coming to pass at such a place— as long as *they* haven't imagined it a different way!

I will make a further comment on the power of symbols. I am encouraging you to stimulate your own creativity. I am *not* encouraging you to follow instructions. Notice that I am not saying, "do this, do that." It is not my job to instruct you. But it *is* my job to encourage you to become. No flower will look ever exactly the same as another flower. It unfolds, it becomes. There is not an authoritarian figure standing over it and saying, "You don't look like the other flower! Back!"

I want to encourage you to become. But I do not want to teach you to be a clone of any one individual's idea of the mystical practices that work for him. Otherwise, what would you be but imitation? No, practice at your *own* creative pleasure.

Stumbling Through a Portal

If one of us should stumble through a portal or doorway, what might we find?

You may find immediately that your orientation has so completely shifted you don't know *how* to move, much less *where*. You will feel completely out of balance because your physical reality will have changed literally 100%. So there will be at least a moment of feeling 100% disoriented.

How do we get out?

Why get in if you want to get out? It is a commitment to go through.

I get a sense that we can stumble through it accidentally.

You could, but it is unlikely. You must remember that you are not here alone. You have teachers, you have protectors, angels, guides, your soul, the Creator. It is not likely that you are going to stumble through, but it is possible. If there were any portion of you on this side, you could find your way back with that portion. Even if you couldn't see, you could *feel* yourself. If you were mostly over there, you would still feel yourself as being solid. You might not feel the reality you are in as being solid because you might be in a transitional space between realities. In that sense, others might see you as a shadow in that other reality.

Let us say that you are in reality A. You find a portion of yourself unexpectedly in reality B. People in reality B might see you as a shadow, or they might not see you at all. People in reality A might simply see, for example, that your foot is still in reality A. They would not see a stump, but they might see a foot. They might, seeing this, become rather alarmed. Chances are, somebody would grab your foot, and they could pull you back, almost like in the movies. However, if you *wanted* to go, all the pulling in the world would not get you back, even if they had a steam shovel there to pull you. They could not do any damage, either. If you wanted to go, you would go.

So I will say it is extremely unlikely. I place the possibility in your head mostly to encourage you to make the motions that are the keys to power.

Could I tie a string of light and then follow it back?

Yes, if you are sensitive to energy, certainly. Chances are that someone would come and find you and bring you back. Some people will help others who are lost that way.

One day I was way up into Boynton Canyon just about as far as you can go, and I heard a loud noise. It sounded like a combination of a strong wind and rushing water. It's not a sound I've ever heard before. Then a few moments later I heard the same sound again. Could you comment on that?

A Telepathic Experience

I'd say that is true telepathy. True telepathy is not really thought. It is your actually hearing something, though others around you might not hear it. In this case it was more of a memory of another time. I know it sounds like it might have been moving through an energy dimension, but that had specifically to do with another time. To build upon that, it is conceivable to have sound as well as sensation when you are around portals or doorways, for example, but it is more likely to be a high-pitched sound.

What are these worlds? Are these possible or probable realities? Are they other dimensions? How can we get a grasp of where these worlds or portals lead to?

Other Worlds: Other Ways of Living Life

A grasp of what they *are* is what I would prefer to say. They are other ways of living life. They are totally different expressions. They are really supporters for you. They are partners and helpers in the creation of your reality. To get a grasp of their reality may be beyond thought, but it is not beyond the joy of emotion that comes as a result of doing something beautiful and delightful. That is the best way to describe it. For you, emotion is the link that ties you between dimensions. You could not be on this planet without being emotional. So it has to do with emotion.

Even though the chances are small, is it possible (either inadvertently or accidentally through some sort of motion) to stumble through one of the pathways or doors? It sounds like certain motions are keys to doing that. So if it's dangerous and not advisable, why do the keys exist?

Keys Exist To Intrigue You

The keys exist so that you will be intrigued. That is why. It is an enigma. As indicated, if you were unprepared when you came back, you would simply be perceived as a crazy person and nothing would be learned by it, nothing gained. It would be a loss. The keys exist so that you will be tantalized to want to pursue it, to want to get through and come back in order to bring back some golden egg of knowledge to pass on to others. They *must* exist so that when the time comes for you to begin all of these spiritual quests in earnest (besides discussing it and acting toward the creation of the experience), these things will be done in public, not in private. Certain individuals will learn to unlock these keys and string them together in the proper sequence. That is the key—the *sequence*. When demonstrated properly, the children will be able to learn how to follow. People who will save the planet (as you understand it) will, for the most part, be from five to seven years old. In other words, they will still be receptive to doing things that are spontaneous. They will not necessarily question too much. And if they are accompanied by others, they will be very brave and adventurous indeed.

Understand that the whole purpose of this discussion is to tantalize you with an enigma. I am saying, "Look at this wonderful world that you have and these wonderful possibilities and doorways, but oh-oh-oh, don't do it!" When you were a child and told, "Oh-oh-oh, don't do it!" what did you do? I understand that you are going to try, and that's all right. The keys exist so that certain individuals will unlock them, and in turn teach them to the children so the children can save your world. It is all like a fantastic story. With that, I will say *au revoir.*

Channeled 3/14/91

Zoosh, I just returned from the Baja where a man takes small groups out for a short preparation and then sends them off separately for seven days to connect more with the Earth and themselves. He's thinking of bringing this to Sedona and has mentioned Mystery Canyon, which he said is next to Boynton. I was wondering if you would say anything about people spending seven days and six nights by themselves to connect more to nature and to the Earth here.

Vision Quests at Certain Vortexes

I think he maybe he means Secret Canyon, because that's next to Boynton. I do not recommend that a vision quest, which is what I would call this, take place in that area. I've heard some people refer to an area in Boynton Canyon as Mystery Canyon. But generally speaking, in the Boynton Canyon, Fay Canyon, Secret Canyon area, I do not recommend vision-quest activity.

This is why: Sedona is laid out, you might say, as a graduate school. There are certain places where one goes when one is beginning to "do" Sedona. When the Native American or tribal populations lived here they would often do vision quests. While I will say that in general, areas in Sedona are good for vision quests, there is a disadvantage to starting out in the area of Boynton Canyon. That is a very powerful energy, plus there are conflicting sources of energy going on there right now. Some things are not welcome in the canyon by the native energies there, and the canyon is attempting to push them out. Other things are very welcome, but they are being disturbed by well-intentioned individuals who are moving things about. Now, when the tribal people came here they knew that the entire area was a vision-quest area. But when the entire area was experienced, say, within a sequence of a vision quest, one did not start out in the Boynton Canyon area. One would complete the vision quest there.

So if your leader wants to have you start out, I would recommend Schnebly Hill, for example. This area is gentle, and there are many gentle places to go there. I know that you have done other things, but even so I do not recommend seven days in Secret Canyon. If it is something that he believes strongly in, I would recommend that he does seven days himself. And if after seven days and nights alone in the area he still wants to bring others and can wholeheartedly recommend people to come in on the basis not only of his growth but on the basis of the love that he experienced there, then all right. But if so, no more than one night for the others.

You see, I'm not saying everything, but this area is very responsive to people's moods. If you are on a normal vision quest—say, for example, on Schnebly—you could have a moment of fear that would pass. It would be with you strongly; you would feel it strongly because the energy is strong even there. But it would pass, and you would perhaps gain from that. But if you were in Boynton Canyon, Secret Canyon, Fay Canyon, all along there, you could have a moment of fear that could become terror and would demand some action on your part.

Now, I know that your leader wants that action from you because he is attempting to elicit from you a total commitment on your spiritual path. But it is not for him to make this demand of you without letting you know what that area has in its potential. So I do not want to set you up one way or another. I will simply say that that area is the *final* step. You can ask your mystical men and women from all different tribes about that area, and I can assure you they will not recommend a seven-night stay there.

A friend of mine was visited the other day supposedly by some extrater-restrials. Would you happen to know anything about that? He lives here in the Sedona area.

ETs in Residence

We'll comment on this exactly this way. "Supposedly" is a good term to use because it is difficult to create proofs. I will say that an individual was visited by beings who live under the Earth. And these beings appear to be from another star system because they have a very similar look to those who are from that other system. It is true that their predecessors were actually from this other place, but they have been here now for more than two generations. So in a sense, you might loosely say that they have become Earth people because they have been established here. It is just that they do not live on the surface.

Can you talk more about that? Are there points of ingress and egress in this area? Are there civilizations...?

One question at a time. There are many different places to move in and out of the rocks. They are somewhat inter-dimensional. That is to say that they are not requiring, we shall say, total spiritual alignment to move through them. But they do require certain gestures, certain motions, and that energy that can be radiated—self-generated, if you would—by the in-dividual to get through. The reason that I say it is not always a totally spiritual thing is that in your civilization there is a ten-dency to believe that all activities relating to interdimensional travel require a high degree of spiritual awakening. But this is not necessarily true.

Technology for Moving Interdimensionally

There are some beings who happen to be living at a quick-er dimension who have inherited certain technology and can move from dimension to dimension based upon that technol-ogy. I want to bring that to your attention so that you do not think that you are somehow the only ones ignorant here—the only "ignorant" ones who cannot physically go interdimen-sional.

But you must remember that when people go through these interdimensional doorways, in the moment of transit through the doorway they are not physical. That's something to think about, because ofttimes I get questions about people who want to move from dimension to dimension consciously. And I say to them, "Well, you do this in your dreams all the time." And they say, "But that's not what I want. I want to do it physically." Understand that you can conceivably take your body with you, but you will have to transform your body into a nonphysical medium, that is to say nonmass, in order to move through these dimensional doorways.

"Animal" Creatures Use Doorways

Now, I mention this because there are what you would call animals that can make these transits as well—creatures, not human beings and not apparently extraterrestrials or even inner-earth beings, but creatures that look more like what you would classify as animals. Sometimes it will be through a portal or doorway or window, whatever you wish to call it, into other-dimensional spaces or into the planet. Other times it will be through an actual hole—that is to say, a cave.

There are many caves in the Sedona area, and some of them have what I would call an access through the back of the cave into a deeper level of the planet. What I am talking about is that you may have to do something to get to the cave, and then you may have to focus your total attention on the idea of moving through into the other dimension. I mention these motions through the access because it is something I did not talk about before when I discussed portals and pathways and so on in Sedona.

Hidden Technology in Caves

It is possible to go back into a cave and find certain grooves, certain holes, even. And by placing your fingers in these in the right space, you can be assisted by the energy that is present there, almost like a code. You can be assisted by that energy to come into a space that will allow you to make the transit into that other dimension.

Understand that it is your tendency when you think about technology to think about a machine, something with moving parts. But technology can also be a rock wall that has certain grooves, certain spaces you use like a keyboard on a computer or even on a piano, and you make the right motions. What this is really doing is training you to make these motions with your hands.

Find the Motions That Open the Door

So sometimes it is fun perhaps to go back there and to try this out and see what happens. If you were to go in those caves and find the proper combinations to go through another dimension, what would you find there? Would you be physically in another space, another time?

You would experience it as being so different that it would seem like another time. However, if you made the physical gestures to get through in this particular cave we talked about before, then you would have done something physical to have arrived there. And while you would have moved through the back of the wall of that cave in an interdimensional state (meaning in an expanded molecular state, a nonphysical state), you would arrive with your physical body. Your physical body would no longer be in the cave, but you would be in a physical world. You might experience a moment of being in a deeper cave in the sense of being very black. Or you might experience little shimmering lights. Or you might experience a light way off in the distance that you would naturally be attracted to. However, you will experience yourself as flesh and blood and solid.

The main thing is that once you've gone through all these gestures to get through the cave, it would be good to continue a gesture. I realize that the audiotape is not picking this up, but I am moving the arms and stroking towards the body and bringing them forward in a circular motion. That works in this way. It is also possible to put one or both hands in front of you and move them out, as long as there is a circle going on, in the sense of encouraging energy to flow through you and out. This keeps you physical. Other than that, you will experience what is right for you.

Possible Adventures

It might be a test, it might be a confirmation of your growth. It might be that you will meet people on the other side. It might be that you will be given the opportunity to stay there for a time. It might also be that you could stay there for two, three, four weeks of experiential time and then choose to go back to your normal life. It is possible that if you were given the opportunity to pass back through the cave into your normal life, you will come back out on the other side having been gone from your own physical time zone for only ten to twenty minutes. You will be disoriented, and yet you will most times have some if not all of that knowledge.

It is true that in the past when people had these experiences, they did not retain all of the information. But they would remember it and apply it throughout the rest of their lives, usually when it was called for or needed. Keep that in mind, because that is not unlike the UFO encounters where people meet extraterrestrials and ofttimes have some interaction with them. Often they will tell you stories about where they've been and what they know. You may not remember these things when you come back to your normal life, but you will remember it gradually throughout your life when you need to know it. Sometimes this is experienced as *deja vu*.

Perhaps an event will happen—not so much a place where you go and remember—a world event, and you will say how wonderful or how unfortunate it was, whatever applies. But after you say it or hear about it or see it or participate in it, there will be a strange sense of familiarity that you cannot place. There has often been a situation where you have been told that a particular thing is going to happen. Perhaps it has been shown to you with a certain amount of forceful impact—that is to say, as a theatrical production, in the sense that you flew into the future and saw it. This is an example I bring forth because ofttimes these experiences correlate with other experiences.

These days it will be different. It is no longer as necessary to forget so much of these things. You can often have the opportunity where you will actually remember the bulk of your experience immediately upon emergence from the other side of the cave. Why? Because you have expanded as a population. Many of you have been on a path of spiritual awakening and have expanded even more in terms of your ability to accommodate new and different ideas and experiences. As a result, it is as if your soul and your body trust each other more and your mind and feelings are entrusted with more of the memories. It is also true that these are such changing times you are living in that you may have need of this information within a few weeks; if not in its entirety, then for many different things in your experience.

So these days it is possible to have this experience on a more fulfilling level, remembering many things. It is possible also to go through the back of the cave and simply have an experience—that is, to go through the back of the cave and feel as if you are floating in air, becoming totally disoriented. But it will not be a negative experience. It will always be something that you can grow with. It will have some way of helping you and those you work and live with and those that you visit in your world.

Other-Dimensional Visitors

You know, when visitors come to your world from other dimensions or other planets they have the same experience. For example, very often in these times there will be a visitor from a planet that is so forward to your own that you might ask how anything they could possibly learn here could be applicable on their planet. Yet there will always be something, if not many things, that they will learn.

Every moment that they spend on this planet, even out in the wilderness, they will have the experience that all of you have in every waking moment and even in every sleeping moment on this planet: They will be immediately thrust into a situation of growth and change. On their planets very often they do not have that much opportunity to grow and change and expand on the accelerated level that you have. Even though they might be using protective devices to create a bubble around them and to keep your world out, still they could not be within the magnetic pulse of this planet without being exposed to growth and change. So they will always have experiences that can enrich their lives and that they can take back and expose their people to so that they too might benefit.

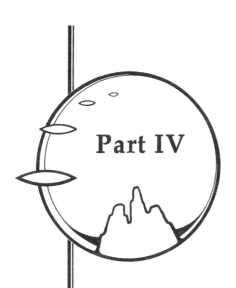

Part IV

CURRENT ET
INVOLVEMENTS

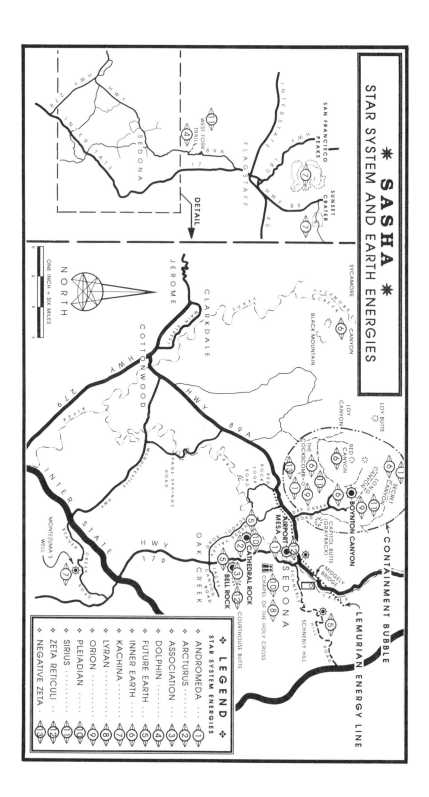

✳ SASHA ✳
STAR SYSTEM AND EARTH ENERGIES

LEGEND
STAR SYSTEM ENERGIES ✣

◆ ANDROMEDA . . . . ⟨1⟩
◆ ARCTURUS . . . . ⟨2⟩
◆ ASSOCIATION . . . . . . ⟨3⟩
◆ DOLPHIN . . . . ⟨4⟩
◆ FUTURE EARTH . . . . . ⟨5⟩
◆ INNER EARTH . . . . . . ⟨6⟩
◆ KACHINA . . . . ⟨7⟩
◆ LYRAN . . . . ⟨8⟩
◆ ORION . . . . ⟨9⟩
◆ PLEIADIAN . . . . ⟨10⟩
◆ SIRIUS . . . . ⟨11⟩
◆ ZETA RETICULI . . . . . ⟨12⟩
◆ NEGATIVE ZETA . . . . ⟨13⟩

DETAIL

NORTH
ONE INCH = SIX MILES

CONTAINMENT BUBBLE

LEMURIAN ENERGY LINE

12

Sedona Energy and ET Calibration Experiments
Sasha Through Lyssa Royal
Channeled 2/22/90

I send greetings to all of you. This is Sasha. May we say that in the first part of this evening we would like to share with you the information that was requested of us concerning vortexes, energy in areas such as Sedona, and the reason why we as physical extraterrestrials use these specific areas for our own purposes.

Presently I am with a group. You would perhaps call it a "mission group" represented by various species within the Association. We are performing calibration experiments.

Let us explain what we mean by that. We are right now in your general vicinity, within what you would call a 30-mile radius. These calibration experiments are being performed between now and what you call the middle of March [1990].

Tapestry of Intersecting Energy Lines

First and foremost, let us say that as many of you know, there are many vortex areas in your world. The question may be asked, what constitutes a vortex area? If you could imagine that your planet is overlaid with a tapestry, a gridwork, you would find that various lines of varying energies would intersect. At these intersection points are what you would label vortexes, energy areas, or power spots. These specific crossovers of energy lines are not necessarily random, but they do not look to the eye (were you to see a grid) to have a certain order. It is very much like a tapestry wrapped around your world with certain threads that intersect. You will find vortex points there.

As you well know, Sedona possesses some of those vortex points. The area you call Mt. Shasta is one as well. There are many, many others in the world. There are several in the United States, Europe, the areas you call Himalayas, and the Andes, etc., and there are areas in Asia. If you were to study the reports of extraterrestrial activity on your world, you would find a greater number of occurrences in these specific vortex areas. We wish to express to you why this is so.

Navigating Energy Currents

We have spoken often about the interdimensional travel of many of the extraterrestrials. Understand that it is a lot easier for you (if you were in a boat) to ride a current than to travel upstream or through dead water. It takes more energy to propel yourself *away* from a current. We find that the currents of energy in various vortex points are cyclical. They spin. Therefore, if you utilize these specific energy points, you can use the momentum of that energy to propel yourself in varying directions and dimensions.

You can then see why interdimensional connection points would be very strong in vortex areas. It would be easier for interdimensional travelers to come through these vortex areas because they can use the momentum of the vortex area to propel them in the direction they need to go. This is the general reason why vortex areas are used by extraterrestrials for travel. It is simply a matter of ease for them.

Specific Color Attunements of Vortexes

If you were to take another tapestry of various-colored threads and wrap it around your planet, you would find that there would be varying congregations of thread colors in different areas. These will symbolically represent the different types of energies that each area is attuned to. For instance, the area called Mt. Shasta is connected to certain energy frequencies; you would find that there would symbolically be a greater number of violet threads in the tapestry that spreads over the planet in the area of Mt. Shasta.

So, in looking at a gridwork of your planet using colors, we can tell which energies are more compatible with certain areas. This can be done for the entire planet, and it can be done for Sedona. Later on we will talk about what your specific tapestry looks like in the Sedona area.

Low Natural ELF Waves Favor ELF Experimentation

In these vortex areas such as Sedona, energy moves outward. It dissipates. Energy moves constantly, always circulating, never becoming stagnant. In terms of the energy that is around you as individuals, you will generally find that the *natural* amount of ELF waves (extremely-low-frequency waves) will be very low in vortex areas. This is why some individuals attempt to conduct ELF experiments in areas with low ELF activity—to see exactly how much they can saturate the vortex area with the ELF energy. So far it has not been very successful, because the vortex activity indeed circulates the energy, always moving the ELF and other waves outward and dissipating them.

Therefore, we prefer to do these experiments (we call them calibration experiments) in vortex areas because the readings we receive are much clearer. There is less interference because the ELF waves are very light in density. Vortex areas are the primary places for us to do the calibration experiments, as the results are very easy to read.

Vortexes Dissipate ELF Energies

Also, the calibration experiments that we do rely on *your* feedback, *your* perception of us. In areas where there is strong ELF activity, you will find that the individuals being calibrated can read *our* energy much less. In that sense, any of you who are somewhat concerned about being bombarded with ELF waves will find it to be eased in areas such as Sedona because of the vortex activities.

The area of Sedona has more than one vortex. It is not just one main vortex, so it is very difficult to ground ELF waves in Sedona. This is another reason why it is very interesting for us to come and do the calibration experiments. You will all perceive us that much more clearer *here* because the movement of the waves is continually going outward.

We Calibrate Our Past Selves Among You

You may ask, "Why do extraterrestrials do these calibration experiments? What are they all about?" Understand that for the most part (not 100% of the time) we calibrate individuals who are reincarnationally connected to us. Therefore I personally calibrate the reactions of this physical channel, who is my past self. Others that I work with calibrate the reactions of their own past selves, etc. So generally speaking, the individuals on any given mission (for instance, those on my craft right now in your area) are calibrating reincarnational connections to themselves. This gives us automatic permission, shall we say.

There are some other individuals who will, on a soul level, give their permission for the calibration experiments. We would say simply that these experiments are *not at all* like what you call abduction experiments. It requires *no* physical contact or communication between us.

Your Response to Frequency Tones

Basically speaking, when we come into the Sedona area (which we are doing right now) the calibration experiments consist of frequency recognition. This means that we will, in your vicinity, focus varying *frequency tones* (interdimensionally speaking) into the general area and calibrate how you register those tones. *We are not talking about tones that will cause you to do anything against your will.* We are speaking of nothing negative. We are speaking of how *you* react to the tones that we give out.

We can do this on varying levels. We can target individuals and give a tone to see how you respond, or we can target an entire town (which we do with Sedona) and see who in the populace will respond. Some of you have noticed that when you get a headache, perhaps 50 other people you know get a headache around the same time. Not that this is always caused by these calibration experiments, but sometimes it can be.

Becoming More Sensitive to Incoming Information

The headache is not the goal of these experiments, but rather it is *your* way of telling yourself you are receiving the energy. In time you will learn how to receive information without creating discomfort in your body. You will become more sensitive to incoming information and need not create a painful idea in order to validate this information.

Thus we use tones. Generally speaking, they are not audible, although sometimes your dogs may hear them.

Broadcasting Color Frequencies for Feedback

Now, we will also broadcast *frequencies within the color spectrum* to see how individuals will react. Again, this will be on an individual level and a general populace level. There are various ways for us to read the specific feedback that we get. Some of it can be read through your own auric-field resonance. Some can be read through your emotional bodies—how you respond to these tones.

Again we will reiterate, we do this *with your permission*. We would not do it otherwise. This is a joint effort between all of us so that we will begin to understand you and you will begin to perceive us. We know that when we do this in these vortex areas, *individuals will begin perceiving us* a little bit more at a time until it becomes more widespread.

Visitors Take Energies Home

The area of Sedona attracts many, many visitors. The individuals that come here will sample the energy. When they do, they will go back to their homes and take a little bit of the energy with them. In a sense, they will create their own inner vortex of energy that they will carry with them throughout their lives. Thus in a sense *they* become targets as well when they move out from Sedona if they wish to continue with the experiments.

When you come to a vortex area and then leave, you take some of that inner knowingness of understanding the vortex and becoming it. This will allow you in your life to begin living as a vortex, to begin circulating energy, to begin processing and moving things through you much more quickly. This is one of the purposes for visiting a vortex area.

Let us speak a little bit about the area of Sedona and the specific energies that are attracted to specific places. Again, if you were to stretch a tapestry over the entire town of Sedona, you would find that various-colored threads (as an example) will gather in specific areas.

Vortex Correlations with Specific ET Energies

For example, the area you know of as **Red Rock Crossing/Cathedral Rock** is a doorway for what you consider to be **Arcturan** and some aspects of **Pleiadian energy**—the feminine aspects. Hence, when you interact with this area, when you open your heart and yourself you will first perceive the more abstract Arcturan idea and then you will begin perceiving, if you wish to go deeper, the Pleiadian idea.

In the areas that you call **Long Canyon** and to some extent **Boynton Canyon** (but not as much as Long Canyon)—in that general area is an interdimensional connection point for **Orion energy**. Understand that when we say "Orion energy" we are not necessarily talking about its negative aspects. We are talking about both aspects. Some of you have had experiences of negativity and fear in the Long Canyon area. This is your tapping into that aspect of the Orion energy. Some of you in those areas have had profound spiritual experiences. That would be a connection with what can be called the Orion Light. It is a different vibration of the Orion energy.

The area you call **Boynton Canyon**, overlapping into **Secret Canyon**, is somewhat intermeshed. The threads are somewhat entwined. You will find a strong Sirius connection there. Again, you will find not a polarity but varying aspects of the **Sirian energy** within that area. Some of you may find what you consider to be the negative Sirius idea. Some of you may find the idea of Sirius that represents your own future selves, your own oversouls. Hence, some of you will have profoundly spiritual experiences and some of you will have negative extraterrestrial experiences. It can range the entire spectrum.

The area called **Airport Mesa** vortex is one (not the only one) of the interdimensional connection points for the **Androm-**

edan consciousness. Within the areas of Long and Secret Canyons there are also Andromedan connections. The energy within the Airport Vortex is considered masculine, electrical, and represents the aspect of the Andromedan consciousness that allows you to begin reawakening very ancient coded patterns within you that go back to creation itself. Hence, those of you that partake of the energies of the Airport Mesa will find (especially if you are fatigued) a rejuvenation. What you are doing is tapping back into your Source—a very primal aspect of the Source in that area. There have been other connection points on your planet for this energy. Some have been considered mythological, such as the Fountain of Youth. This would be that idea translated somewhat differently.

The area called **Bell Rock** represents many different ideas. It is a crossroads for many different threads on the tapestry of the connection points for Sedona. You will find that in the Bell Rock area there will be a large degree of **Association of Worlds** activity. Thus you will find many different beings of many different species interacting in that area. You will generally find them along a *specific* frequency. You will not often find beings of the lower densities within the Bell Rock area. Those would be more comfortable being within the Long Canyon area. Every once in awhile, a lower-density being may pass through the Bell Rock doorway, but it will not remain in that area very long.

Vortexes Cycle Their Leadership

We would say that within the Sedona area, although there are a varying amount of vortexes, there is a cycle that occurs as to which becomes the main pulsing vortex, as it changes intermittently. We would say that for the time being the Bell Rock vortex can be considered the "leader" in terms of vibrationally setting the pace for the rest of the vortexes. We speak of the present, and we sense this has been true for at least the past year and will continue for some time. This is so, simply because you are all allowing yourself a certain amount of integration not only within yourselves but with your other selves in other worlds and dimensions. This specific vortex area represents that integration of yourself on many levels.

A New Doorway Near Midgely Bridge

There is also what you would consider to be a minor vortex area that leads up the canyon [Oak Creek Canyon] toward Flagstaff. You can say that the entrance point to this vortex is not linear, in the sense that you can walk up to it. The analogy we would give is that you have to come to it at an angle; it is not accessible from the road. You would have to walk somewhat. It is within a half-mile radius of Midgely Bridge.

That particular energy, for the time being anyway, represents a *new doorway* that has opened, which is allowing many playful beings from other realms to enter the Earth-plane consciousness for the first time. This is partly why we say that you have to approach it at an angle. As many of you have suspected, Sedona exists somewhat within what you would consider to be a bubble. Many of you, while you are here, feel as if you are living in this bubble—somewhat secluded but at the same time somewhat safe. Hence, beings that come from other universes and other dimensions who wish to experience the Earth-plane consciousness will enter through this doorway, which is somewhat insulated, that allows them access to Earth-plane consciousness but from the bubble of Sedona—somewhat protected. That is what we mean by "coming in at an angle."

This particular doorway is open to all those who are curious about the Earth-plane consciousness but to no one of a negative nature. So if you wish to play with this idea, we would suggest that you go out to the area of Midgely Bridge. Follow your nose, as it were, and explore. Find the surges of energy. It may be very subtle, depending upon the "traffic" that day. However, you may begin to sense various beings (not only from this galaxy but from others) passing through. You may, if you wish, be like the hula girls with the leis when they come through —and welcome them to the Earth plane. You can extend a hand, if you will. That was the analogy we came up with!

The Chapel Area

We wish to talk a little bit about the chapel area. It is not in and of itself a vortex. However, it possesses a strong electromagnetic field that can at times generate interdimensional doorways. There are various beings that will primarily use the doorway in the chapel area to come through into the Sedona area. Very often myself and many of my comrades [Pleiadians] use this area as a primary entrance point.

When you say you use it as a doorway to enter, what do you mean?

There is not a doorway in the rock per se; however, the interdimensional doorway that would take us into your reality, the one that is most aligned with our energy, is in the chapel area.

Do you mean you come through that doorway when you are channeling?

No, when I come physically in a craft. It is an area that resonates very strongly with **Pleiadian** and (to some extent) nonphysical **archetypal Lyran energy**.

Would you say the actual structure of the chapel is close to this point?

Yes. Between the chapel and the back wall of the canyon as it curves around, the doorway will shift, although it is primarily in that area and somewhat past the chapel. If you were going down the road to the chapel and were able to pass the chapel and keep going straight and veer to the right, that is also another strong area for us. The imprints in the field of Sedona have allowed that area to be a resonant area for us. We primarily use that point. Sometimes we will use Bell Rock.

Would you say the chapel itself would be appropriate for meditational purposes? Or is there too much tourist energy?

We would say that you would find a high increase in energy should you wish to meditate in that vicinity. The chapel itself is located in a spot that focuses energy like a lens. It would be perfectly fine to go there. The only time it may get a little too much is when there is an entire busload of tourists. Other than that, it is a very powerful spot. When the native humans were living in Sedona in the past, that was one of the areas they considered highly sacred. This is carried into the building of a church there.

When you visit Sedona in your craft, do you get out and walk around?

We do not get out and walk around at this point. As I speak to you now, I have stepped upon your world twice. Neither place has been an area of great population. Once it was in the Andes and once on a remote tropical island in the south Pacific.

The Zeta Reticuli—you didn't mention them. Do they use all the vortexes?

It depends on their "mood"! (That is somewhat of a joke. Do you get it?—not that they have moods!)

Give me a moment to answer that. I am with four other beings presently, and I am constantly being fed information. If you can, imagine being with four other individuals who are all talking at once, and you are having to translate what they are all saying simultaneously. This is what we are doing.

Bell Rock and the Zetas

The area you call Bell Rock is a primary travel point for the **Zeta Reticuli**. It depends on the orientation of the specific Zeta Reticuli race. It has been said that there is a negatively oriented Zeta Reticuli. Those specific individuals would come through the Long Canyon area. The more benign Zeta Reticuli will come through the Bell Rock area and sometimes the Airport Vortex area as well—generally those two points are for the more benign ones.

West Fork and the Sirians

What about West Fork? It is about 12 miles up Oak Creek Canyon.

That area in and of itself is a playground for dolphin energy. It is also a nonphysical fifth-density entry point for **Sirius consciousness**.

Any comments about the Schnebly Hill area?

Schnebly Hill, a Doorway to Future Consciousness

Yes. That particular area, interestingly enough, is a doorway for what you consider to be consciousness from your future Earth—when you harness time travel you will be visiting all the new agers "back when." That is a doorway they use. The future Earth idea also uses Bell Rock and Red Rock Crossing.

Do all Pleiadian energies coming through that Schnebly Hill area represent our future returning?

Yes. Let us say one thing first: Though we have given you specific areas in Sedona and their connections, it *does not* mean that another being cannot come through those specific areas. We are giving you a generalization of the energy. However, beings can use *any* doorway they wish.

The future Earth has a heavy Pleiadian cultural exchange going on, as well as one with the hybrid species [Zeta-human]. Because they are there on the Earth in the future, you will find those consciousnesses mixed together.

Yes.

You have said some things that I do not understand. You said that in your incarnations you are connected to us—are you our future?

Yes! I personally represent a future life of this channel within the Pleiadian system. I am a future life of hers. My civilization for the most part represents you in the future, in the sense that many of you will choose to have future lifetimes in the Pleiades.

Vortex Diameters

Are vortex diameters constant? Is there a realm of diffusion? Or does it vary with each one?

It varies with each one, and each one will also change. There is not a consistent diameter. It is similar to the idea you call tides in your oceans, as well as riptides, if you will. Though you can find certain cycles, there is not necessarily a set pattern. They do change. A lot depends upon how much energy you put *back* into the vortex areas, how well used they are by consciousness, etc.

Great Pyramid Linked to Bell Rock

Recently I received some information that there is a direct energy link from Bell Rock to the Great Pyramid. Do you have any comments on that?

We would say that is accurate. There are other direct connection points, threads on the tapestry, that are connected to that specific pattern. The Bell Rock and Great Pyramid connection also connect to other areas as well.

What stimulates so much past-life recall in Boynton Canyon?

Boynton's Past/Future Connections

Boynton Canyon *does* have a very strong Orion connection (as do many of you), as well as the idea that is called Sirius both past and future. The past Sirian connection for you represents certain patterns you've had in your Earth lives playing out Sirian energy, especially some of the old-god karma that was played out on your planet. It also represents your future. So when you go through the vortex areas in Sedona, you are somewhat bombarded with the energy of your past *and* your future.

I live in an area called "Kachina" about five or six miles from the Boynton Canyon vortex. I've heard that the vortex expands all the way to the area in which I live. Could you comment?

Smoothing Those Energies

Yes. The area that you live in, in a circle pattern around the Boynton Canyon perimeter, is somewhat of a containment bubble. Many of the individuals that live within the Kachina area (which includes where you physically are right now) are helping to balance the energies of Orion and Sirius that are infused in the Long Canyon/Boynton Canyon area. Many of you who live in these particular areas are actually assisting in balancing and smoothing out some of the rough edges. This is why many of you are consciously and unconsciously attracted to those areas—to do that very thing.

The area where I live seems very gentle and mild to me. It seems like there are pockets of that type of energy in Sedona as well.

A Fault Line Described

Yes. We will state that you live somewhat parallel to 89A at the junction of Coffeepot [Drive]. Understand that there is a line of energy that runs east from the area west of Sedona parallel to and south of 89A. This line of energy runs from West Sedona all the way up the [Oak Creek] canyon. There are various pockets of energy along this line that in some places will seem very intense and very unpleasant. There are some that will seem very peaceful and calming, and some that will contain both. This is related to the ancient Lemurian idea, when this area was submerged and was a playground for many dolphins. That particular line of energy [fault line] was activated at the "destruction" (though it was not just one momentous event) of Lemuria. That was one of the areas where the plate began disintegrating. It has begun healing again, but there is energy there that represents many different emotional ideas.

When I first got here, I felt a lot of dolphin energy.

The Dolphin Connection

There is a strong dolphin connection here, mostly in your linear past when this area was partially submerged in water. There were many dolphin creatures that existed in this area. In very ancient times dolphins were the primary form of life here, along with other etheric beings. You may also be picking up on the Sirius connection.

Do you want to comment on how seismic activity relates to the locations and fluctuations of the vortexes?

Seismic Activity and Vortexes

Very often you will find that there is somewhat more than normal seismic activity in areas where there is vortex energy. As many of you know, there is a volcano that last erupted somewhere around 1100 A.D. in the area of Flagstaff. You will find that at times, in terms of energy, eruptions will take place in some of these vortex areas as a bleeding off of energy. If the individuals who inhabit that area and if the ecology of the area it-self do not provide a natural circulation of energy, it will get bot-tled up and may manifest as volcanic or earthquake activity. You find this occurring at times in the area you know of as Hawaii, Alaska, and the Andes, which are also vortex areas.

I've heard a lot of predictions recently about volcanic action in the fu-ture in the Flagstaff area. Is it something that is going to happen, or something we can keep from happening? Is there anything we can do to smooth that energy out?

You are doing it now, in terms of smoothing the energy out. We perceive the possibility of volcanic activity, but not a strong *probability*. If you continue to do what you are doing now, you will naturally circulate the energy and thus not need to create an eruption from the inside of the Earth.

When you say "you," you mean the people in Sedona as a group?

Yes.

Crystal Cities

Are you connected with, or do you know about, any teaching done by Pleiadians in the so-called crystal cities here?

The crystal cities you speak of exist within fifth- and sixth-density realities. Therefore, they would be considered to be etheric. They are populated by various beings, but there are in-dividuals here from my civilization (fifth and sixth density). Understand that when you get to that density, you lose a con-nection with the idea of "civilizations."

During the past couple of days I've been very aware of some of the ener-gies that are being projected in. When we feel we are being zapped with those energies, is there anything we can do in terms of a response that would be helpful in your work? Are you looking for any particular responses from us?

What To Do When You Feel Our Energy Projections

The optimum response we would like to see (were we to create a response ourselves) would be that if you feel us present, if you believe that we are calibrating, sit quietly and perceive as much as you can. If you perceive color, consciously make a note of it. Really, the optimum idea is for you on a *conscious* level to take note of what is occurring—not that you have to go running around telling what happened, because it is a very private experience. But allow the energy and the recognition to filter into your conscious state. That is what we consider a breakthrough to the layer of physicality.

If you feel discomfort, we would suggest (if you are willing) that you go to a specific area in Sedona that you feel drawn to in that moment, an area that will heal you. More often than not it may be the area called Red Rock Crossing. However, do not be surprised if it turns out to be an area such as Long Canyon. Where you feel you want to go will be exactly where you *need* to go. This will assist *us* the most, which will in turn assist *you* the most.

Are there particular times when you do the calibrating? Three or four in the morning or the afternoon? Is there any particular pattern to it?

Generally speaking, we will calibrate you when you are awake and engaged in relaxation, but not usually when you are engaged in work. That would mean meditation, socializing with your friends, whenever you are relaxed. We will also do a recalibration in your dream state. That is the primary way we do it. What occurs is that you go through the motions in physicality of pretending like you don't know we are there, and then in the dream state we all sit around together and laugh over how you did such a good job pretending we weren't there!

What do you mean by "calibration"?

Calibration—Measuring Your Responses

Calibration simply means measurement. We measure your responses, emotional responses, to stimuli. We often leave the emotional testing to the Zeta Reticuli. We don't really need to understand your emotions, for some of them are like ours; we are very much alike. It depends on the specific group that is involved. For instance, there is one being in the group that I am assigned to right now who represents the Zeta Reticuli race. *He* would be interested in calibrating your emotions.

Nobody does calibrations without a larger end in view. Is the purpose for which you are doing this essentially learning how individuals here will be most likely to have conscious, clear reception of information from you and others?

Yes. It is not only for the optimum purpose of allowing you to get used to the idea of other aspects of consciousness (i.e., extraterrestrials) and therefore begin to manifest it in your daily life. It is also for the purpose (for *you*) of beginning to recognize your own guidance and unseen influences. It is not only so that we may begin to communicate openly; it is also for you to be able to grow in your own intuitive nature. Ultimately speaking, the greatest desire within the Association (if we could say the Association has one "emotional" desire) is to interact openly with you. Because of this "emotional" desire they hold themselves back further than perhaps they feel they need to. That is a little secret.

Does the calibration process utilize the implants that we may have?

The particular group that I am involved in does *not*. There may be some "etheric" implants (which in no way react as foreign objects within your auric field) that are placed there for temporary purposes. But we would not consider them to be implants in the way that you understand implants.

Future Submersion?

I've seen some extensive channeled information [in the form of a chart] about Earth changes. According to this information, these changes will be triggered by major events in Nevada and California starting in 1992. They talked about Sedona over a period of the next 5-10 years becoming submerged by substantial water of the Pacific Ocean. Can you comment about that?

Yes. We will *never* invalidate information that has come from other sources. We would say in the light of this that it is, of course, a possibility—as *anything* is a possibility. However, in terms of reading the energy, we do not perceive it will be *necessary* for you to create that. Hence, we would say there is not a strong possibility.

The Calibration Team Described

Now, some of you have asked about the calibration and also who is involved. Understand that various species will do the calibration for their own purposes. The specific group that I am with now represents four different races. Basically speaking, each race will have its own area of interest. Each individual will calibrate in their own area of interest and all of the information will go into what you would understand to be a data bank within the Association. The data will then be used later to understand the mass-consciousness patterns of your planet and also to calculate the higher probable realities—not by mathematical formulas but through energy patterns.

The group I am with now represents two Pleiadian beings, male and female (myself being the female). There is an individual from the culture you know of as Essassani, which for all intents and purposes is a cross between humans and Zeta Reticuli—a hybrid. There is also an individual that is within the Zeta Reticuli line, though his genetic structure has been changed slightly so that he can interact with the more humanoid races. Finally, there is an individual from what you call the DAL universe, an interdimensional universe.

You have a DAL there now? Male or female?

Female. Those of you who have read the Billy Meier material on your world will find that race to be familiar. Basically speaking, they are a race that exists interdimensionally. This is difficult to describe, but they exist between galactic consciousnesses. My race very often will engage in interactions with the DALs to learn much. They have much experience technologically, psychologically, and in many other areas.

It is obvious that the Zeta individuals would be interested in calibrating the emotionality of the individuals they work with. The Essassani being would be more interested in calibrating your mentality. My specific interest is in the psychological responses to stimuli, the changes in auric energy and everything right down to body posture. The DAL individual works much with the outward energy in areas like Sedona to variously position the craft in such ways as to maximize the usage of the energy [in a vortex area]. In this case, she is the navigator/pilot. The other individual is a male Pleiadian by the name of Jagar who serves as an etheric historian. He is needed in this type of calibration to understand the past and the futures of the individuals who are calibrated. He also works very closely with the Essassani being.

Is the Essassani being anyone we know?

No; but as you say, they all look alike!

Can you get very specific and describe how a vortex works? How does it interact with the energy of someone who comes to it?

Vortex: An Intersection of Different Time-Space Continuums

Understand that when polarities meet, there is a change and a *third* idea is created. You follow?

Sure. Third vector.

Basically speaking, in a third-density reality in a linear time-space continuum you will find that intersection points of varying time-space continuums will create the energy similar to *two threads of opposite polarity.* (At this moment, I am translating what is being said to me.) Hence, in terms of a vortex, the primal creation is of two separate lines of energy that interface and *thus create a third changed or mutated idea of the two.* Do you follow?

You have a horizontal and a vertical and they meet.

That is *one* idea.

So that is one dimension. Does it go through the Earth also?

Antimatter and Black Holes

Those would be considered different types of energy points. They would be considered more as nexus points, in the sense that they will condense in on themselves and in some instances create what you would call an antimatter flip—like a cone. For instance, if you have a cone, what you see at the surface of the planet is the outer or top of the cone (the wide portion). The energy of the cone funnels itself into the Earth to a very condensed point. Depending on the specific vortex, it may or may not condense itself into what can be considered (in space) a black hole and flip itself into an antimatter universe.

There are varying ideas of what these two specific points are that become a third. You can also say that layer upon layer upon layer—many different ideas: vertical/horizontal, time/space, gravity/its opposite, matter/antimatter—create the twine that in turn causes the lines [of energy] that cross. You all understand that analogy? The different layers we have mentioned make up the threads in the twine that in turn make up the rope [of energy lines] that crosses [into a complex gridwork]. These are various things that make it up.

Your Polarized Universe

You all exist within a polarized universe. That is what you've chosen to be a part of for this existence. Hence you will find that your interaction or interface with reality is based on polarized laws. You will find that the specific vortex energies are created by the mixture of these different polarized ideas which have created the threads that make up the ropes [or lines of energy] that cross. The crossing points are the vortexes.

Vortexes will shift along your planet, though primarily they will stay in basically the same area. When you as human individuals enter a vortex area, you begin to touch some very primal ideas within your own nature—your own dualistic nature, your own yin/yang, your own very primal polarized ideas. Many of you who travel to vortex areas will find that you are forced to face aspects of yourself. You will find that various things happen in your life, sometimes with great rapidity, so that you will be forced to come to terms with these portions of yourself in order to integrate, and to create by this integration a vortex within yourself. You will thus *become* the vortex. Then when you leave, you carry the vortex with you. You become a minivortex. You assist others who come into contact with you to find their own vortical energy. This is another way to achieve the transformation into fourth density.

Are these vortexes in Sedona integrating into one vortical spiral?

We perceive at some point in the future (perhaps in the next 100 to 200 years) they *may* become one vortex. The possibility is strong.

Is there an overlapping of the energy? I almost feel (like when I am in West Sedona) that there isn't anywhere that I don't feel the energy.

Zones of Neutrality

Yes. There are overlaps at times. Again, it will depend on how they pulsate. There are overlaps and buffer zones, or zones of neutrality.

Where are some of those?

There is a zone of neutrality between one-half mile from the entrance of highway 179 (from I-17) to the area just before you are able to see the red rocks. That is a neutral zone. This means that it is without vortical influence, and some of you may use it to experience a great amount of clarity and inner peace without external influence.

You say the zone starts a half-mile from the freeway. Does that imply that back toward the highway there is vortex energy?

Yes. The area you call Montezuma is also a vortical energy that is *different* from Sedona but just as powerful.

Can you comment on areas such as Montezuma's Well and Rimrock?

Kachina Energy

Those specific energies—Montezuma, Sunset Crater, San Francisco Peaks—represent (as the Native Americans call it) kachina energy. *Kachina energy represents a unified tapestry of extraterrestrial energy.* Understand the analogy that we have given you of the tapestry. When you stretch the tapestry over Sedona, you find a pattern of different-colored threads representing different frequencies. The tapestry will be somewhat uneven or haphazard. You will find, if you stretch tapestries over the areas that represent kachina energy, that the threads in the tapestries would be symmetrical. That is the difference.

You touched a little bit on why there is such a wide variance of experiences in the vortexes for different people. Would you say something about how we can maximize their experience in a vortex area?

Maximizing Your Vortex Experience

Yes. First of all, when you enter an area such as Sedona, you insert yourself into a primarily fourth-density vibration. Therefore, your "rules of life" (according to third density) such as time and expectation, will somewhat be altered, to say the least. If you wish to partake of the vortex energies, enter the vortex areas *without expectation* and without a time frame. This will allow you to absorb the energy and to utilize it in a way that is best for you without conscious interference. Do you follow?

Yes. Except for what you meant by without a "time frame."

Meaning, "Well, I have only an hour to spend in this vortex. Let's see if I can really *make* something happen in this hour."

Inner Earth Linkages

Do any of the vortexes in Sedona have linkages into inner Earth?

We would say that the primary linkages to that area would exist within what you call Long Canyon, Secret Canyon, Boynton Canyon, Sycamore Canyon and Red Canyon.

Government Access

Does the government or any aspect of it have access to these?

Not those, no.

Which ones do they access?

Of those related to inner Earth (in the sense of the consciousness that inhabits inner Earth) you will find that the government is not *really* a part, in terms of usurping those linkages. They are aware of it, but they are also aware that for them, to venture there is dangerous. The portals seem to shut. Some people have been lost in the portals.

Do the ley lines pass through the Earth, or are they only on the perimeter?

Vortexes: EM Frequencies One Mile Above and Below the Surface

Generally speaking, you will find that there are versions of ley lines within the Earth that correspond somewhat to the ley lines on the surface. They all join together at the Earth's core, which is an interdimensional portal as well. However, speaking primarily in terms of vortexes, you will find the ley lines that you are more interested in on the Earth's surface to be an overlay of electromagnetic frequencies that lie between approximately one mile beneath the earth to approximately one mile into the atmosphere.

It is in the primary magnetic field, then?

Yes.

Do the vortexes facilitate our being able to bridge consciousness across into fifth and sixth density?

They can, yes. They help you to achieve an altered or expanded state of consciousness.

It is like the way all these groups are coming to us—a two-way door, right? A meeting point? We have access to other dimensionalities more easily in a vortex.

And they have access to *you*. That is primarily how we can get to you—by riding those currents.

In the way that we speak about probable futures, can we also speak about probable presents?

Yes.

And we can speak about the "accuracy" with which energy can be characterized. There may be varying opinions on what the various energy systems around Sedona and the planet look like. Is it accurate to say that it is sort of up for interpretation?

Yes.

Vould you say that your picture is a highly probable picture, as opposed to saying it is 100% accurate?

We would say that *for us*, our picture is *very* probable! How is that for a very safe answer? You will find that a consciousness (as is its nature) will read an idea according to its own belief. If you have individuals or consciousnesses who are highly paranoid, you will find they tend to concentrate on what is *wrong* and protect themselves from it rather than concentrate on what is *working* and what can work even better. So it is really a state of perception.

The more powerful the vortex is, the closer the nexus point is to the intersections? Is a cone there?

Yes. We would say that the more powerful vortexes are the vortexes whose nexus point (the bottom of the cone) is closest to the Earth's surface.

Okay, there's a cone. As with cones on the physical body (in the chakras), is there an inbreath and an outbreath? Is there an exchange of energy? Does it come into the Earth at that point? What is the energetic flow?

A Vortex Outbreath and a Probable Reality

There is an exchange of energy (we will call it the outbreath). You will find that this exchange of energy will lead to a probable-reality structure at the other end. What does this mean? As a mass consciousness, the choices you have *not* made exist in the outbreath.

So what is in the inbreath, then?

The inbreath is the entrance into your reality of energetic influence from the probable reality at the other end of the cone. There is an energy flow in and out. You will find, however, that it is not contained between those two polarities, for each one can also birth another. Therefore you find a grand matrix is created, rather than simply two cones end to end.

If four visitors came to Sedona to go to the vortexes, and one wanted spiritual expansion, one wanted mental clarity, one wanted emotion-

al balance, and one wanted physical healing, could they get what they wanted from any vortex simply out of their intent, or would they need to go to specific vortexes for their particular purpose?

Specific Help from Specific Vortexes

Good question! Ultimately, wherever they draw themselves to, they will get what they need. Many of you might say that this philosophy is a spiritual cop-out, but that is our answer. The individual *will* be activated, no matter where they go, on the level they *need* to be activated.

For instance, if someone comes to Sedona to experience psychic activity, past-life revelations, and they've read their books and *know* they must go to Boynton Canyon to have the experience they seek, they may try to get to Boynton Canyon every day and never make it! But they always seem to end up down at Red Rock Crossing. You will find that the conscious mind may actually be a deterrent to the inner process that occurs when someone comes to Sedona. That is why, in answering the previous question, you [would best] let go of all expectation. *That* is when you will get what you really need.

We will take your question a step further and simply say that if someone wants **mental clarity** we would suggest Airport Mesa vortex as choice number one and Bell Rock as choice number two.

If someone wishes **physical healing**, we would suggest they combine Red Rock Crossing/Cathedral Rock with the Airport Vortex.

If someone wishes **spiritual insight**, they may utilize Cathedral Rock. They may, if they wish, go to Boynton; the area of Montezuma's Well will also assist.

Emotional clarity you will get just about anywhere. It depends upon *how* you wish to experience it. If you wish to experience it with a great amount of drama and emotion (tears, etc.), we would suggest Bell Rock. If you wish a calm, nonintrusive and very loving interaction, try Cathedral Rock. It depends on what you are seeking. Some of you like to purge and get all of the emotion out—Bell Rock would be the place.

Montezuma's Well

Regarding Montezuma's Well, there seem to be two distinct areas. One is the well itself and the other is a few hundred yards down at the creek. Could you comment on either one of those places regarding its vortex energy?

The area of the well can be considered a self-contained vortex, in the sense that it is very balanced and does not lack a polarity. As we have said, it also represents the Kachina consciousness (or the symmetrical tapestry). The creek area you are speaking of represents more of a bridge between vortexes and not a specific vortex itself.

You said before that it was best to come into a vortex without expectation, but I still wonder if it is important to work on our own motivation.

Motivation and Expectation

Motivation and expectation are two different ideas. Motivation is the energy that allows you to move outward, the energy that allows you to create action. Generally speaking, those who come to Sedona will be highly motivated. Now, the motivation does not have to be connected to the expectation. If you find that you are coming to Sedona because you are motivated to experience a physical sighting of a spaceship, you will find that your motivation and your expectation are connected. However, the idea that will allow you to get the most out of [being in Sedona] would be for you to encourage your motivation to move into your expectation of simply *being*—living in the moment. Therefore, expectation is not present and the moment is what occurs. The motivation fuels you from moment to moment.

Can you speak of the usage of vortexes for specific purposes?

Experimenting with the Vortexes

If you wish to perform certain experiments within the vortex areas, you will find the success of the experiments will be correlated with your *need* for them to occur. More simply, when you wish to experience something in a vortex because of an emotional *need*, you will find that the emotion in and of itself will propel you to experience what you *need* to experience, not what you *think* you want.

If you are clear in your emotionality and what you wish to accomplish (not out of an emotional need)—which is why some of the Taoist and Buddhist practices may assist you—then you will find high success because you stay focused.

Could you expand on the nature of the grand matrix? You mentioned earlier an energy configuration like a grand matrix.

The Grand Planetary Matrix

The grand matrix of your planet may seem haphazard to the eye. However, to many who study it there is order within the chaos. Some of you know there is a science called the science of chaos [chaos theory, or nonlinear dynamics] that represents the idea of a grander order beneath apparent chaos.

Therefore, were you to view the giant matrix, or the tapestry, you would find that at first glance it would seem haphazard. But then you would find that there is order within it. You would begin to see why certain energies enter your Earth plane in these different frequencies and wave forms. You would begin to understand why it occurs. You would begin to see the movement of these energies and to discern a pattern in the movement. This is very multidimensional and abstract. We would simply say, rest assured that in chaos there is always order.

If you were coming into this planet from out of the system (I am assuming within this dimension) and you saw the Earth turning on its axis, how do you focus when you want to come to Sedona? What is the process with which you aim? Is it intent of thought? Is it navigational skills?

Navigating from the Pleiades to Earth

Understand that I will answer differently from others, depending upon the specific species usage of propulsion. I am not an engineer, but I will relay to you how we in my culture achieve the movement from the Pleiades to Earth.

Basically, we make a jump, a folding of time, a tesseract. We make the jump from my time in the Pleiades to the congruent time on Earth—your future. The first jump will be to the future of Earth. Once I am in the orbit of your future Earth, I will shift the time continuum (or my own personal time continuum) to *your* time. In that sense there is a twofold movement.

Once I am in your time, the recognition of various vibrational patterns from various places on your world will act as a magnet to draw us in. There are various areas on your world that I visit most frequently. They are logged, if you will, within the structure of my craft. My craft will respond to those electromagnetic pulses.

So are you saying that it is an emotional coordinate?

Yes. We would say that at my level of technology in my civilization now, we cannot travel anywhere that we do not have an emotional connection to.

Do you mean the future or one possible *future?*

Possible Futures, Possible Pasts and Probable Realities

We do possess the technology to travel to possible futures, yes. In that sense, when I travel from my time to your time you are a possible past. I am a possible future to you.

When you make that jump, do you hit the same future every time?

In the beginning of the experiments in my culture, it was common for navigators to get lost in probable realities to the point where they could not get back because they could not keep track of where they *were*. Therefore, we have structured our entire travel ability around the idea of making emotional connections with our target point. The emotional connections act as a homing mechanism, and therefore we do not get lost.

What was behind my asking that question was this: Is there a consistent probable future, or does it shift and change depending upon what is happening?

There *is* a consistent probable future in the sense that I can return time and again to you, to your life and energy line. But I can also return time and again to your probabilities. There has to be a point, however, where we allow ourselves to not explore. Understand that we are not all *that* much more advanced than you.

Why did you choose this particular probable present of ours? Do you have a similar group in other probable presents?

The Crew Members' Local Connections

I chose this particular probability because this person [the channel] exists here. The person that this person chose to be was what I needed, or was what I wished to experience. I chose this probability because this channel chose to be who she is in this lifetime and we could thus work together.

So Lyssa is the emotional connection you have. What about the other four?

The other Pleiadian has a connection in this time-space. Each of the others on the ship also have connections within what you call the southwestern area of your United States in this time frame.

Flight Time from the Pleiades

In Earth time, what is the subjective and objective time it takes to jump from the Pleiades to here?

Subjective from my point of view would be the blink of an eye, a breath. Objective...from whose point of view?

Yours.

If it is from mine, then it is subjective.

How long would the people age in the Pleiades while you were gone?

It depends on *when* I return.

Sasha has the option of returning at the same time that she left.

Traveling in Pairs

Understand that in my society when we time-travel, we do it in pairs, meaning that one person stays behind. If the individual does not return instantaneously, we know something is wrong, because the person will always target the return to one second after departure.

You could be experiencing millennia out there while you were gone!

Yes.

I've asked Sasha how many people live on her planet and she wouldn't tell me, because it changes each time she comes back. The number changes because a lot of Pleiadians are time-traveling and some will show up and be on the planet.

Did you say that you travel only in pairs?

Yes. But we mean that one goes and one stays behind.

Is that necessary on large operations like this? I mean, you probably have at least one mothership out there from your time.

It is not necessary in this particular instance, because you are dealing with the Association. This is not considered time travel. Time travel in the sense you are referring to would be considered one person going back into time and physically interacting for a specific reason on the planet. That would be considered time travel. To us this is not time travel.

You may ask, "How do you stay consistent in your own reality? How do you know when to have a meeting?" Understand that when you exist outside of time, you develop your own version of time, your own consistency. You really begin to experience the idea of the Tao or of synchronicity. That is truly how you must live to be able to exist outside of time.

In a sense, as long as where (or when) you are going feels normal or natural, it is not considered time travel. So you can go to our future Earth and then come here. To you [Sasha] they are two different planets; emotionally they are two different places. But if you were to go ten years into our past, you might have to use your standard time-travel precautions.

There is ultimately no difference between the distance of this chair to that table and the distance to Alaska in terms of space. It is the same idea as you have just described. There is no time difference nor incongruity between twentieth-century Earth and twenty-first century Earth, from my point of view. They are merely places like two different closets you would open.

Since it is so easy for you to time-travel, would you consider going, say, ten years into the future for specific individuals you are calibrating? That might give you a faster way of doing what you are doing now.

We *do* do that! Thank you for the suggestion! We need to do the calibrations *now*, however, because of the transition on your world. *This is the time.*

We are at a nexus. We don't have a definite future that they can look into. The future Earth Sasha refers to is not necessarily our future. This is why they can so easily go to both places. But our resultant future (from what we are doing now) is what is unclear. There are a number of different tracks open.

For a closing idea, what do you have planned tonight?

Calibration.

Who? What? Where? When?

Tonight's Calibrations

Remember, we stated that we prefer to do two phases of calibration—one in the waking state and one in the dreaming state. We have done the waking-state calibration of all of you. Tonight we will do phase two. Each of you may experience many different things from subtle to blatant. It doesn't really matter whether you remember a thing.

Just simply know that you are loved greatly. We appreciate your willingness to join us in learning more about life, God/All That Is, and ourselves. We send you our love and our appreciation. May you have sweet dreams.

13

UFO Encounters in Sedona
Joopah and Zoosh Through Robert Shapiro
Channeled 7/16/89

I [JOOPAH] will begin by saying (speaking for my people, the Zeta Reticuli), that we have had less activity recently in this immediate area. We have been called elsewhere.

Andromedans and Others from the Farthest Reaches

However, other groups are now involved here much more. Amongst them are Andromeda and several from the farthest reaches of the galaxy, for which you have not developed any names. Perhaps they are free to name themselves. There is a great deal more activity here than there was before, but the Zeta clan is involved elsewhere, for the most part. However, we have some assistance programs associated with the other groups. That is to say, very often on the Andromeda ships they might have one or two of us to assist them. Perhaps the biggest change here in terms of the vehicles that have been present is that there are fewer but much larger vehicles. In the past there have been many small vehicles around this immediate area, but now there are perhaps three or four quite large, dominant vehicles. They hail from various places in your universe, but generally they are from an area you are familiar with in your study of the stars.

The Vehicle from Sirius

There is one vehicle from Sirius, but not anything to be concerned about, because it is filled with beings who are associated with the development of the Sirian water people here.

To be specific, many of you know that dolphins and other sea creatures hail originally from Sirius. These beings have a source, meaning that on their home planet they do not appear as they do here. It is just that mankind is here to resolve not only their own lessons on the soul level, but also to act as a clearing house to resolve lessons from many of the nearby star systems and planets unable to work them out for themselves. Thus what you have come to call "karma" is really the inherited lessons from others who have been unable to deal with them.

The Sirian vessel that is here, then, is really the source of these water creatures. On their planets they are beings having much the same stature as yourselves, meaning that they have a body form that is more humanoid. On this planet, of course, they must take these various shapes you have come to refer to as animals so that they will not in any way conflict with the idea here that mankind is the dominant species.

This Sirian vehicle, which I will describe simply for your edification, is one that would seem to you to be wet. It is damp inside almost all the time, and there are pools of water. The water is a little different from your water, more akin to what your scientists have come to call heavy water. Yet it is filled with life forms. The people who occupy it might, from your point of view, swim from place to place. It is, in a sense, an ocean in the sky. Yet they are humanoids—two arms, two legs and a head—some of whom in variations could pass for human.

There are many other beings living in this star system of Sirius, but I mention this one to clarify the idea that the so-called animals here are really derived from this source being. They are here primarily to make a final study of your oceans during the current change that your planet is developing. Mother Earth is getting prepared to expunge many of the discomforts—that is to say, to clean herself. So there is what you might call a last-minute check on the status of the oceans as well as the lakes and the rivers, but it is a secondary check to be done, since they are already there.

Parked Above Sedona

You might wonder why a water vehicle is parked above Sedona. "Parked" is the term. It is never very far from here. Of course, it is sufficiently far in the sky to not pose a threat to navigation; and of course it is also usually invisible, only occasionally allowing portions of itself to be seen when those portions can appear to be stars. They have a very long vehicle, about ten miles long. And sometimes just for fun (which is their way, since they are amusing), they will allow a light that is quite bright from where they are but (depending upon your point of view) can be seen only from underneath.

These vehicles have the ability to create what would appear to be optical illusions, but they are quite real. They will sometimes, just to be funny, allow this light to move with the underside of the vehicle, creating what briefly appears to be a satellite moving across space. Of course, you must allow for certain distances and know that if you see something that moves from one side of the sky to the other, it will be a satellite. But if you briefly see an object that moves rather slowly, like a satellite, and then disappears, even when you allow for the range of optical situations, remember that they have the ability to alter optics.

Thus one might experience them in unexpected ways. It might be the Sirians kidding around, suggesting that, well, they are humorous. This is *almost* a breach of the intention to remain anonymous, you see—but it is so cleverly done that the Network allows them to get away with it, since it really causes no harm. It is very much like a satellite in appearance, but it will appear for only a short duration in space. I mention that simply because some of you might see it if you have not already done so. It is, in fact, here.

The vehicles are involved in the future work that will develop here. This area, as stated several times before by Zoosh and others, will in time be a water area. It is, even now to the casual observer, a place that has in fact been a water area once upon a time, but it is again developing. There is no immediate reason for people who have a home in the hills to build a boat dock in their front yard, since this will take quite a bit of time, in terms of experienced time.

Preparations for Earth Cleansing

The beginning work is being done. It is being done in synchronistic activity with the Mother Earth, who prepares herself for this cleansing. The cleansing operation will happen somewhat interdimensionally, with the assistance of devices that can neutralize many forms of polluting substances that would otherwise take many, many years to break down. I must say, however, that the radioactive pollution will, for the most part, not be altered.

You must understand that you are in transition from one aspect of this planet to another. When that transition is sufficiently completed, you will not really experience radiation, but you will unfortunately leave it behind for those who inherit the third-dimensional aspect of this planet known as Earth. Your race has been thoughtlessly disposing of much material into the oceans, and we foresee a major radioactive leakage that will seriously contaminate ground water.

The inheritors, however, have been experiencing negative energy for a very long time. When they come here and experience any positive energy at all, it will be quite a wonderful thing for them. So even though the planet will be mildly radioactive and have outbursts of that from time to time, their bodies are a little bit more durable and will therefore be able to tolerate this condition, unlike your own bodies. Indeed, the radiation will be deemed a plus for the new inhabitants. So while there is some assistance to Mother Earth in her cleansing from extraterrestrial sources, there is also a certain amount of noninterference as well.

I mention this Sirian vessel because there has been so much talk in the past about this negative planet from Sirius and its connections to you. I want to remind you gently that for the most part that planet is the exception, you see. Other beings from Sirius—the source of dolphins, whales and so on, the source beings—are present. They are here. If you feel their energy (which is possible), that is why.

I saw what appeared to be a ship last night. I was wondering if there is confirmation of that, and if there is, where was it from?

This appearance (I do not wish to hurt your feelings) was just that, an "appearance." Become aware that there are also certain energies in this area that will sometimes create the appearance of something that is not always real.

Last week about 8:40 p.m., I went out into the yard. There was an object that came in from the northeast, made an arc to the southwest, and went back in the direction it came. It seemed to be very large and glowed, but there was a period where lights were flashing off of it in an erratic pattern. In looking at it further, it looked almost like the lights were being reflected off points on its surface. As it turned and went back toward the northeast, it made no noise. But it appeared there were two high-speed interceptor planes taking off after it. I've never seen anything quite like that before. I wonder if you can shed any light on it.

Government Testing Hybrid Vehicles

Thank you. This type of experience will become more common. Be alert to the fact that you are somewhat in a flight zone for the testing of what will begin to be called in time "Earth's flying saucers." There is being developed now a very gentle relationship between certain forces on Earth and beings from elsewhere. This particular vehicle has been here before and will be back. The vehicle will ofttimes disguise itself in ways that will be similar to a plane. Sometimes it will make no noise whatsoever, since it has that capability. But it also has an auxiliary power capability that will sound suspiciously like a plane. In other words, what you have here is a test vehicle that has more than one motive source.

This is not what you would say a false sighting, but it is a sighting of, we shall say, the presence of space technology within an Earth vehicle. Your government has recently stated that it will begin public testing of this so-called Stealth bomber and such business. That is a front, a cover because they are really beginning to test their new vehicles, which look very much like what you've come to call flying saucers. It is not, contrary to some people's opinions, an intentional cover-up to be able to say, "See, this is what flying saucers are all about," though some people will pass that information about. In reality, this is the beginning of public contact. It is your government's way of preparing the citizens to accept that there are civilizations elsewhere.

I do not wish to seem as though I am breaking faith with government officials with whom I and other members of my race have been in contact, but you might say that government officials have felt that it would be of value to release this information through highly unofficial sources. You might say that from the governmental point of view, allowing for my GS rating, *I* am simply an "unofficial source." So I will simply say that you have seen a vehicle that could be called "hybrid technology."

In the last few weeks there have been a number of people suffering from chills and fever. Are there any particular influences?

Ultrasounds Associated with Earth's Cleansing Preparations

Thank you. This is not associated with that extraterrestrial source. It is a little bit more associated with adjustments to the frequency intensity that is involved in Mother Earth's work. I might say, as an aside, that there is a support effort from extraterrestrials to calm the energy. I do not want to leave you with the impression that extraterrestrials are interfering with what Mother Earth does, but in order to cleanse herself she must intensify various sounds that are primarily ultrasonic. However, these sounds have a deleterious effect on the surface population. It is not possible to totally rid these sounds from the surface, because they must be there so that Mother Earth can do what she must to cleanse herself. But there is some attempt by extraterrestrial sources to nullify the sound sufficiently so that people will not have more than minor discomfort. A good question.

I had heard several years ago about there having been in very ancient times a dolphin temple in this area. Earlier this year, I was up there with a friend, and we had an experience of a dolphin being (but not in a dolphin body) who took us into this rock whose inside looked like a temple. Can you tell me anything about that?

Chapel-Area Temple in the Rocks

As stated at the beginning of this evening, the vehicle that is the source of that dolphin energy is not only conveniently parked above this area, but requires that there be corresponding underground circuitry here, of course. As you know, underneath the planet there is a considerable amount of underground activity, and beneath this particular locale there is more than under many other places. There are windows, one might say (portals is perhaps another word), to enter these quicker [higher frequency] dimensional areas. Depending upon your frame of being and your cultural reality, you will perceive, if given the gift of entrance, different sights inside.

Your experience of the temple had to do with the natural arc of your soul's experience through this planet. In a sense, what you were seeing was not something of the present, but more associated with the past. Since this area is in time going to be under water, it will become a treasure house of reverential or sacred objects of the sea or ocean. These objects will be utilized to condition, harmonize, or tone the aspects of this planet, which will move from the third dimension to the fourth dimension. When you saw that temple, you were actually in view of the ideal that will be created but that was associated primarily with the past.

What is this energy that is in my house and how was it put there? Is it an entry into another dimension?

A Crack in Time at Home

You are referring to something that is rather personal, but it has reflections in the community. You are referring to what amounts to a tunnel, almost like a crack in time. It was there, of course, before the structure was built. But the structure is not so much of a monument to present architecture as a monument to that of the distant past, emulating architecture that flows with nature rather than that designed to conquer nature, as it were. I mention this in the context of what we are discussing tonight, because this crack in time will move about somewhat, and sometimes give the impression that it is some*one*, rather than some*thing*.

This will also have effects in the community. It is not exactly extraterrestrial, but it is balanced from extraterrestrial sources so that it does not become a problem. It creates windows, of course, through which you will have occasional experiences that seem bizarre or abnormal. But it will also cause this area to be seeded with an energy that allows it to be much more magnetic and much more electrical than the area might normally be. The structure of the ground, the iron content, largely has to do with the doorway that this represents. It is somewhat involved, of course, with the interdimensional experience, and it is tempered largely through the use of inner Earth and extraterrestrial balancing techniques.

Can we presume that the more positively polarized ETs will tend to not reveal themselves out of respect for noninterference and, conversely, the more negatively polarized might tend to intervene more in this third dimension?

This is a duality question. Since the original statement of the question was "reveal themselves," and the second aspect of the question was "intervene," you understand the question is worded a little off there.

Well, "reveal" implies intervening by altering our belief system.

The original status of the question, however, was noninterference. So I will simply say that regardless of the beings' positive or negative status (referring to the actual statement of the question), the intent to reveal may or may not be allowed. If there is a negative desire to intervene, there is no more permission than there is for the positive. So, no not really. It is just that it is more likely, as you know, in your civilization for the squeaky wheel to get the grease, yes? That which is unpleasant or uncomfortable will receive much more attention than that which is pleasurable. This might occur in a simple relationship, where it might sometimes feel like the relationship is all wrong, whereas there is really only a brief moment of discomfort.

Primary ET Portal

Is there a particular place in the Sedona area that is a primary portal or connection point for extraterrestrials?

I will point you in the direction and let you find it on your own. If you perceive up Oak Creek Canyon, as you say, past the place where people playfully slide in the water [Slide Rock State Park], you will feel an energy from your right. Find the spot. That is all you get!

Very often in Sedona I see what I call "cloudcraft." They always have a specific swirling shape; sometimes they are very large and sometimes they are very small. I want to understand what it is that I am really seeing. Is it a being, a consciousness, or a craft?

Cloudcraft from Arcturus

There is, of course, a natural phenomenon in this type of cloud, but I will simply say that when the cloud is unmistakably shaped like the vehicle you have come to know as flying saucer and it just sits there, as they will, acting very uncloudlike, they are very often just what they appear to you to be. But sometimes when they have the vague shape about them, they are simply the phenomenon of lenticular cloud. I will say, however, that when the former happens, it is a somewhat borderline interference that the network allows, since this type of cloud does exist. It is a simple case of allowing oneself to be seen when one could be mistaken for something else. Yes, there are beings on board and these are vehicles, but only when they look quite obviously like them.

Are they from a particular planet?

Very often they are from Arcturus. This is not a planet; it is a star system, but I see no reason to say the names of these planets, because most of the time they are unpronounceable in your language.

Is the primary purpose of Bell Rock an energizing point for UFOs in this area?

Bell Rock Navigational Beam; An Overhead Vehicle

That is not the *primary* purpose. It is what one might refer to as the secondary purpose. A left or right turn signal on the car is like that. It is not the primary purpose of the vehicle to flash that light, but the flashing light on the car allows it to tell others where it is going and, in a sense, where it has been.

So one might say that the navigational beam produced at various times of the day, especially in the evening, by this particular rock is an auxiliary or ancillary purpose.

ZOOSH: Zoosh here. My friend Joopah has been called away to activities elsewhere.

One night while sitting at Bell Rock, I saw above the rock what I thought a city of lights would look like.

People have indicated that there is a city above this city. This is true on an interdimensional level, but what you were experiencing was something that was a gift, as visions can be for one individual and not everyone. But this was, in fact, a vehicle. It is difficult to grasp that they can be so big, but they can. You will know it is a vehicle when there seems to be a distortion in the fabric of space—that is to say, a ripple effect. This was a vehicle that you were allowed to see.

In August 1982 a friend and I went up to the Airport Road. I wanted to show her Sedona in the evening. This UFO came out of the southeast, went across 89A and behind Old Greyback [Capitol Butte], the mountain. It had no lights, it looked like a cup turned over on a saucer, and it was a luminous, greyish pink apparition. She looked at me and I looked at her; we had both seen it but we could never discuss it. Was that something that we manifested?

Waving at the Zeta Ship

It was real. I might add that the source there was Zeta Reticuli, and there is a reason for not having discussed it. I will say, by way of suggesting alternatives in your mind, that it was not the first time that both of you had seen it. It was, speaking allegorically, as if you had some friends over on a Sunday afternoon and they said goodbye and hugged you at the door and walked down the street to their car. They couldn't park too close to the house, you see, because the people across the street were having a wedding when you asked them to come over and many cars were parked there. But you were sitting on the porch and a few minutes later your friends, having left, got in their car, drove by your house, and waved in a friendly fashion. I will not say the exact sequence was so immediate as that, but the allegory is appropriate.

About a year and a half ago I saw this craft. It was shaped like a boomerang and was bright orange. Could you tell me where they were from?

The Orange Boomerang

This was a very opportune sighting. Normally, this color is broadcast by the Zeta beings, but there is a craft referred to as the "V." Because of your particular locale and because of the energies and the optical effects of this area, you saw this vehicle as not being as big as it actually is. But it was the *original* vehicle that came here from Sirius to create the human race on the genetic level. It was available for sighting by several people; it was sighted by a few, but not many.

14

Sedona, an Ascension Center
Jørgen Korsholm (Jananda)

In 1985 contact was made with me by Serapis Bey, the Ascended Master who is responsible for planet Earth's and mankind's ascension to the kingdom of everlasting peace, or fifth-dimension frequencies. During a meditation he appeared and told me that he and I had work to do together. My response was, "How wonderful! Please give me more information." "Wait and see" was his answer.

Arriving in the United States in 1989, someone gave me *The Ascension Handbook* by Tony Stubbs. Beginning an enthusiastic study, I received permission to translate the book into Danish and sent it to friends in Denmark. I used its information for my own ascension work. My ongoing work with Serapis Bey had begun.

Serapis Bey recently informed me that he came to planet Earth from the Central Sun in the Pleiades a long time ago to serve the cosmic plan of evolution. His function was to serve as the Sun god Ra, and in many other incarnations as an Egyptian pharaoh. The Solar Brothers were later told to withdraw their energy to see how mankind would respond to the power and responsibility given to them. As has happened everywhere on Earth, the priesthood kept the knowledge exclusive to themselves. When conquering invaders later arrived, the secret records—and the potential of empowerment through the knowledge—was thus destroyed, depriving both the elite and the people and delaying the evolvement of mass consciousness.

Serapis Bey Ascension Flame Arrives

In February 1991 the Master informed me that he had moved his Ascension flame from the temple at Luxor, Egypt, to Sedona, where I had relocated about nine months earlier. I was contacted around four o'clock in the morning (as was normal) and shown an enormous spacecraft of unusual form about to land in the vortex area of Cathedral Rock. On its top was a 45-foot high, fourth-dimensional crystal about 9 feet in diameter and shaped like a rocket the color of an amethyst. It was placed below, and centered between, the two outer rock towers, as viewed from Red Rock Crossing. (Anyone standing at that location can see a gray-colored pyramid within the color of the red rocks. If one looks 30 feet above that within the rock structure, one may be able to see the color emanation of the crystal.)

Responding to my inquiry, these space beings informed me that they were Solar Brothers from the Central Sun in the Pleiadean system. They were transporting the crystal from Luxor to this particular vortex so that its energy could support the planet in its ascension process. Great changes were going to take place very soon both here and in Egypt. They also told me that people visiting this area hereafter could more easily make their personal ascension; it would be enough just to be near the vortex for a short time. The radiation from the crystal would help quicken the necessary changes in the body, especially now when this galaxy is entering an area of very high Light frequency.

Imminent Change for Cathedral Rock

On March 12, 1991, I was informed that during the following July or August a storm in the Sedona area will cause electrical energy to surge from Bell Rock and Airport Vortexes (both electrical) to Cathedral Rock at the apex of this triangle, transforming its energies from magnetic to electromagnetic. This will be part of a basic shift in the energy of the Earth's magnetic grid. The ley line coming out of Cathedral Rock extends to the Azores, Glastonbury, and to the island of Iona off the southwest coast of Scotland. (A group of White Brothers in a monastery on

Iona have meditated at noon daily for several thousand years, as I was told by a personal friend who had visited them, to energize Earth's grid with the incoming energies from the galactic center.)

This and other changes in Earth energies are in preparation for a shift of the magnetic north pole several degrees closer to the geographic north pole. This in turn is a preparation for a shift of the geographic poles that will hopefully come in small stages.

Human Tampering with Earth's Magnetic Field

I had an earlier experience during August 1989 when I was staying in Oak Creek Canyon north of Sedona. I was awakened early one morning and, in a nonphysical state, transported in a spacecraft to the Nevada nuclear test site, where I suddenly found myself in an underground bunker with seven people and a great deal of electronic equipment. Just as suddenly I was back in the ship watching red lasers trace a huge U within the earth, creating a powerful energy field. It was explained to me that imminent tests would endanger San Francisco and Los Angeles and that this field would prevent a manmade catastrophe. The open end of the U, pointed in the general direction of Portland, Oregon, would divert the blast energies into the North Atlantic. He said to me, "We don't want a catastrophe to occur *now*."

As early as the thirties and forties, the Space Brothers were aware of man's dangerous tampering with the atom. After the U.S. and other governments decided, against their warning, to build nuclear plants all over the Earth, gigantic spacecraft had to be stationed outside Earth's atmosphere at certain positions to balance Earth's precarious electromagnetic field structure.

I was told that every nuclear plant seriously unbalances the magnetic field within at least a 100-mile radius. For instance, a nuclear facility in Arizona, located only 55 miles west of Phoenix, is causing a structural change in the magnetic field in that area, which is resulting in changes in the weather patterns. This sort of distortion is the reason that enormous crystals (far larger than the 45-foot one described above) are being placed in certain areas. The Phoenix-area distortion naturally affects locations adjacent to it, including Sedona, which is close to the edge of the radial influence.

ET Intervention to Balance Earth

Both spacecraft and crystals are being placed in locations to keep Earth balanced. Much activity is taking place presently because of the imminent adjustments she must soon make in her field. If the situation becomes serious enough, there may need to be intervention by extraterrestrials seeking to preserve Earth. Extraterrestrial engineers and scientists are keeping close watch on this and other areas.

I believe that the two crafts I saw at about 7 a.m. April 16 (1991) may be related to this. The first, coming from the north, had a unique shape: a ring about two miles in diameter. A few minutes later another unusual shape appeared, extremely flat for its enormous width, with only a small convex shape on its top, metallic in color. On April 18, in the early morning again, I conversed with a space being whose body was the form of a clear crystal about my height. He said his group was from a crystal planet in the Pleiades. The Crystonians, as they call themelves, are here to help balance Earth's electromagnetic field by placing crystals below the surface where needed. He suggested that humans can communicate with earth crystals as intelligences who can assist them.

July 11, 1991

The solar eclipse coming up on July 11, 1991, will, I think, have an important effect not only in the area of Cathedral Rock, where I have observed the activities noted above, but upon human consciousness itself. The energies of such an event have great influence but are little understood. The July event is a preparation for the **11:11 Doorway**, a major shift that begins on January 11, 1992, and will last a number of years. These years are the time period humanity has to become single, united in its consciousness, for only that single Being may pass through that doorway. Let each of us truly let into our hearts Love and Light.

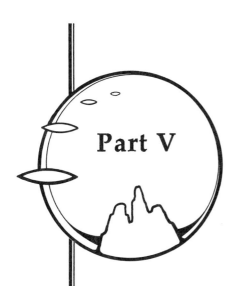

Part V

A MORE PHYSICAL/ EVOLUTIONARY VIEW

15

An Overview of the Geophysical Aspects of Vortexes*

adapted from a paper presented at
The 1982 International Conference of Meta/Geophysics, New York
with an added section describing
The Vortex at Sedona, Arizona

Alsgoud Sprinke

Definition of a Vortex

Vortexes (the scientifically preferred form of the plural) are swirling masses of pure energy, rotating about an imaginary axis that extends through the Earth. Rotation may be clockwise or counterclockwise for each associated energy type, and is dependent upon the total interaction of all geo-energy fields. Rotation may reverse, usually instantaneously and without prior indication, as a result of the constantly changing variations in the interaction of the Earth's geo-energy fields. Rotation reversal may occur repeatedly. It is normal for two vortex axes to experience rotation reversal simultaneously.

The energy associated with a vortex may be of any type, but will be of the same type over the whole axis. A vortex axis may have more than one type of energy associated with it; those energy types will be compatible over the length of the axis. A vortex axis may or may not have a positive and a negative pole, depending on the predominate type or types of energy associated with that vortex axis. The term "vortex" is commonly used by the public to describe one end or pole of a vortex axis.

Vortex axes always pass near, but not necessarily directly through, the center of the Earth. An axis may be bent, as the lineal path of each is affected by the interaction of all and by the Coriolis force. Therefore, the opposite poles of a vortex axis will be approximately opposite each other on the Earth's surface, but not geographically directly opposite in all cases. The path of each vortex axis through the Earth is affected by the paths of all others, and by the changing energy fields.

Vortex poles move over a period of time. They may migrate in one general direction, or ay rotate over a circular or elliptical path. The path of pole migration may or may not be predictable, and is determined by the interaction of the separate functioning fields of the total geo-energy field of the Earth.

Vortex poles are not marked by any standard or notable physical distinctions on the Earth's surface. They can be located only through empirical geo-energy measurement, using available technology. The energy types known to be associated with vortexes are gravitational, magnetic, astrometrical, electrical, thermal, psychic, atomic, natural, cosmic, kinetic, and potential. In addition, there may well be others not yet discovered.

A given energy type may be either emitted or inducted at a vortex pole, but not both. Energy is emitted at a positive pole and is inducted at a negative pole. Vortexes may have one positive and one negative pole, two positive poles, or two negative poles. A vortex axis which serves two or more different types of energy may have different combinations of positive and negative poles for the different types of energy. The total entropy of the Earth's system approaches a stable state.

Energy emission or induction at the vortex poles may be sharply delineated at the Earth's surface, or the flow of the associated energy may be diffused through a number of different channels in the vicinity of the vortex pole. Diffusion may occur at one or both ends of the vortex axis. Diffusion channels are affected and defined by: geologic features, such as rock fractures or faults; land mass variations, such as valleys, mountain peaks, or bodies of water; and man-made channels or obstructions, such as cities, road networks, or great structures.

Geophysical land masses, for the purpose of this work, are defined as any land mass rising above sea level, and therefore contacting the atmosphere. One end of the imaginary axis of a vortex will always be found within the boundaries of a geophysical land mass; the opposite end may emerge under an ocean, or may also be found within a land mass. The energy associated with a vortex pole located under an ocean will attempt to find a path to the atmosphere through a diffusion channel in some nearby land mass, if possible. The poles of a vortex may always be precisely located through geo-energy measurement, but diffusion channels and surface exits are unpredictable and difficult to locate or measure precisely.

Diffusion of energy at the poles of a vortex axis does not in any way reduce the strength or effectiveness of the energy type. The strength of the energy associated with a vortex axis will be strongest where it exits to or is inducted from its form in the atmosphere. The total quantity of energy available at a vortex pole, however, will be divided over the number of diffusion channels through which the energy travels. The amount of energy available at each diffusion channel exit at a given vortex pole will not necessarily be equal.

The Vortexes of the World

Twenty-two vortexes, constituting the poles of eleven vortex axes, have been identified worldwide. It is not known whether or not all existing vortexes have been discovered; however, no identifiable pattern seems to exist that might yield any new vortex discovery, and geo-energy measurements appear to indicate that the mapped geo-energy fields of the earth are complete.

If other vortexes do exist, there must be a sufficient number in proper juxtaposition such that the combined energy flows and fields yield a balanced input to the total entropy of the Earth. It is quite conceivable that others remain to be discovered. Researchers have been concentrating in two areas: throughout the Ring of Fire, the belt of volcanic activity that encircles the Earth; and in locations of ancient civilizations that appear to have been receptive to the fields of geo-energy.

The approximate locations of the known vortexes of the world, which are the poles of the vortex axes, are listed as follows, with the pole located in the northern hemisphere named first. The nearest land mass exit is listed for oceanic vortex poles, rather than the exact geographical coordinates, with the exception of the north geographic pole, which is marked precisely on virtually all maps. The vortexes are listed alphabetically, to avoid the appearance of importance of any one over another:

Angkor Wat, Cambodia – Machu Picchu, Peru
Bermuda, Atlantic Ocean – Stirling Range, Western Australia
City of Refuge, Hawaii – Kalahari Desert, Botswana
Great Pyramids, Egypt – Tubuai Islands, South Pacific
Katmandu, Nepal – Easter Island, South Pacific
Mihintale, Sri Lanka – Galapagos Islands, Pacific Ocean
North Geographic Pole – South Geographic Pole
North Magnetic Pole – South Magnetic Pole
Sedona, Arizona – Amsterdam and St. Paul Islands [Indian
    Ocean]
Stonehenge, England – Stewart Island, New Zealand
Ulan Ude, USSR – Tierra del Fuego, Chile and Argentina

Effects of the Sun and the Moon on Vortexes

Many forces and energy types are associated with the Sun and the Moon, including all of the energy types associated with vortexes. However, the effect of gravitational force far overshadows any other effects produced by the two bodies. Both the Sun and the Moon exert a gravitational force on the Earth, and both affect the energy fields associated with all vortexes.

Gravitational force is an attractional force by its nature. The force, and hence the effect, of the Sun is, of course, much stronger than that of the Moon. In general, the effect on the vortex will become stronger as either the Sun or the Moon approaches an overhead position, and will be strongest when both are directly overhead, if possible due to the geographic location of the vortex. The effect of either body is weakest when it is over the opposite side of the Earth.

If the pole of a vortex is emitting energy, then the emission will become greater as the Sun or the Moon approaches an overhead position. If the pole inducts energy, then the induction force will become weaker as either of the two bodies approaches overhead.

For any individual energy-emitting vortex, energy emission will be strongest when both the Sun and the Moon are as close to overhead as the geographical location of that vortex will permit.

For any individual energy-inducting vortex, energy induction will be strongest when both the Sun and the Moon are as close to being overhead the opposite pole of that vortex axis as possible, given the geographical location of the vortex axis.

The amount of Sun- or Moon-induced variation in the energy emission or induction at any vortex is dependent on a number of factors. The amount of variation may be calculated through empirical geo-energy measurement, using available technology.

The factor having the most effect is the geographical location of the vortex, which determines how closely overhead the Sun or Moon will pass as they continue in their predetermined orbits. Other factors are the type of energy associated with that vortex, the number of energy types associated, the elevation of the land surface, and the surrounding topography. The amount of the variation will also vary with the time of the month and the day of the year, as the trace of the orbital paths of the Sun and the Moon move across the Earth's surface.

Astronomical Effects of Vortexes

The energy emitted from or inducted by vortexes is measurable from outer space, defined as all space at that distance from the Earth's surface that extends beyond the troposphere. The accuracy of known geo-energy measurement techniques decreases as distance from the Earth's surface increases.

The effect of vortex-associated energies outside the immediate confines of the Earth's atmosphere is miniscule, as measure don the scale of the Universe. The total of all vortex fields of energy constitutes a geo-energy system which is largely confined to the Earth, although a small quantity of various types of energy is lost to space, inducted from space, or used in balancing energy forces located outside the atmosphere. Examples of each are: radio waves beamed outward; light waves received from other star systems; and gravitational balancing with the Sun, Moon, and other planets.

The geo-energy systems of the Earth have virtually no effect on the Universe outside the solar system. However, as stated above, geo-energy is measurable from outer space. Given an instrument of sufficient sensitivity, the emission and induction of energy types at vortexes could conceivably be detected at distances barely within comprehension.

It is certainly plausible that if there are intelligent beings attempting to make contact with us from somewhere beyond the solar system, they are homing in on the vortexes as recognizable points of tangency to this world. If they are advanced enough to have developed interstellar travel, then they have undoubtedly also developed instruments capable of detecting and measuring our geo-energy fields and their vortexes, and are capable of sensing these fields and vortexes for use in directing whatever navigational and motive devices they may utilize.

Effects of Vortexes on Life Forms

It is well known that the concentrated types of energy that exist at a vortex do affect life forms, including human beings. The consequence of such effects is beyond the scope of this work, which is intended to discuss only the geophysical aspects of vortexes. There are numerous books, articles, pamphlets, and other written material describing the results of the effect of the vortexes on life, and particularly on humans.

Life forms in the immediate vicinity of a vortex, or the exit point of a diffusion channel of a vortex, will absorb an amount that is greater than normal of an energy type that is emitted from that vortex. If the vortex inducts an energy type, then a life form in the immediate vicinity will experience a reduction in its normal component of that energy type.

It is interesting to note that ancient civilizations, in a number of cases, seem to have recognized the locations of vortexes and to have been drawn to them. It is generally assumed that these people did not have instruments capable of geo-energy measurement.

The Sedona Vortex

The precise point of exit of the vortex pole located at Sedona, Arizona, is 34 degrees 51 minutes 6.1 seconds north latitude and 111 degrees 47 minutes 25.3 seconds west longitude. There are numerous diffusion channels in the area due to the geologically fractured and sculpted nature of the rock formations and the existence of the subsurface Oak Creek geological fault. These diffusion channel exits are found both close to and as much as 50 miles away from the true pole of the vortex axis; however, of all the known vortexes, this one probably has the most concentrated area of diffusion.

The opposite pole of this axis emerges under the Indian Ocean, at an estimated 36 degrees 40 minutes 11.6 seconds south latitude and 71 degrees 20 minutes 19.2 seconds east longitude. The nearest land mass exit point is Amsterdam Island, and diffusion channels exist throughout the Amsterdam and St. Paul Islands.

The types of energy associated with the Sedona vortex are gravitational, astrometrical, electrical, psychic, natural, cosmic, and potential. This is more than the average number of energy types associated with a vortex axis (the average is three). It is known to be a positive pole for the astrometrical, electrical, psychic, and cosmic energy types.

The pole is known to be migrating in a northwesterly direction, but at a very slow rate. The speed of pole movement has been estimated to be just a few inches per decade. The lack of historical data prohibits accurate measurement or prediction of the movement.

Archeological data seems to indicate that pre-European civilizations were cognizant of the geo-energy fields existing at this vortex. Numerous settlements and sites of probable religious derivation have been located within the diffusion area, and appear to be concentrated at the diffusion channel exits.

Energy fields and levels at this particular vortex have been closely measured and have become the subject of much research. The results of numerous studies in the geophysical, psychic, physiological, and geo-energy measurement regimes, have been widely published in many languages. Such material is beyond the scope of this work, which has been restricted to a broad overview of geophysical aspects. It is the author's hope that the reader has been given a better understanding of the mystery of vortexes.

16

The Nature and History of Vortexes

Nova 8

Vortexes, simply put, are spiraling streams of energy that contain within them the Light patterns (codes) which define creation. When Light is first cast forth from the Source, it interacts with itself, dividing into various rays or "properties" as if it were passed through a prism. Specific properties are then redirected based on their ability to contribute to the manifestation of a desired experience. Manifestation occurs as soon as the properties or rays of Light are projected (focused) by way of vortexes and made to intersect with one another, forming a holographic image. Be it in a brilliant star, the miracle of the human body, or a gently rolling stream, everything is created by Light.

Altering Light Projections

In order for a created image to have a life span, the Light projections must remain constant in all respects. When the projection is altered, so is the creation and, subsequently, the experience. And, like television, as long as there's an energy supply an image will remain. When it is time to change the station and move on to another experience, the Light projections can be altered in several different ways, either individually or collectively. The major tools for change include: (1) realigning one or more of the vortexes, which may affect the relative location of the image as well as its design; (2) adjusting the vibratory frequency of the patterns by stepping down or amplifying the

Light projections (adding or subtracting the number of filters, so to speak), which adjusts the density of the form; and/or (3) varying the Light values/rays within the vortexes by increasing or decreasing certain properties and/or their intensities, which influences the creative expression as a painter would do with a brush.

Tracing Earth's Origin from Its Vortexes

The origin of all creation, whether it be the human structure with its chakras or a planet with its sacred sites (areas where the vortexes intersect with the surface of the planet; the locations of the 12 + 1 *primary vortexes* are encoded in Numbers 2 in the Old Testament) can be traced through its vortexes. Planet Earth resulted from the convergence of 12 + 1 primary vortexes which represented all patterns of creation ever experienced by the many and one Universe. Each vortex, containing a specific ray of Light with its full spectrum of expression, was directed by the Creators and guided through specific star systems until it intersected with other vortexes at an agreed-upon point in time and space. When this took place, an identifiable field of energy (a Light pattern or "planetary grid") was established, taking the form of what is now recognized as a paradise planet. As seen by the Creators, the vortexes appear as great arcs of multicolored Light corkscrewing back and forth along interstellar pathways (cosmic highways, so to speak), and converging in a ball of rainbow essence before returning to their Source.

To experience the vortexes, allow your Self to be drawn to a location that you naturally prefer. These "natural attractions" occur because the Light properties are also a part of the human encodement. Therefore, each soul has a corresponding relationship with a specific ray and vortex. Those who are in harmony with the Light patterns will be magnetized to the vortex which matches their personal encoding. To be in harmony is to be in step with one's natural order of evolution and synchronized with the flow of Universal events. By exemplifying only Love, being free of fear and doubt and open to change and acceptance of others, you will greatly enhance this process.

For those interested in information relating to one's personal relationship with the Light patterns (the templates defining sound, color and numerical sequence/mathematics manifested within the DNA matrix of the human vessel), it can be accessed by way of meditation, contemplation, or other inner personal methods. These codes reveal not only the blueprint for one's role within the planetary program but the pathway for soul evolution beyond the third dimension.

Locating One's Natural Home on the Planet

Many individuals are now locating their "natural" homes on the planet as we enter this final period of transition. Such periods occur when an energy configuration of a particular existence passes and a new image takes its place (likened to an ice cube melting into a pool of water). The vibratory frequencies of Earth's elements are now being raised, reducing the density/ limitations of the matter and expanding states of consciousness (awareness of one's existence and environment) of the souls embodying it. All third-dimensional energy patterns (whether physical manifestations or thoughts held within the mental, emotional, and astral bodies) are now being stimulated to support the soul's journey through the may dimensions of the Universe.

The Encodings of the Thirteenth Vortex

The thirteenth vortex, identified as "+1," holds a special role in Earth's period of transition. It is sometimes referred to as the energy "capstone," for not only does it contain all encodings of past and present planetary cycles, it also holds the activation codes that initiate the final sequence of events for the ascension of the planet into the fourth dimension and beyond. It is here that a new Light pattern is being projected that provides for the transformation of all that exists within our present reality. This 13th Light pattern is equivalent to a grand tuning fork that resonates the vibratory frequencies represented in the fourth dimension so that all third-dimensional creation can tune to the next octave of existence.

Entities who visit...vortex sites will be affected in some way by the higher frequency Light projections. If not in harmony, they may feel somewhat out of sync, to say the least. But once attuned to the energies, they will begin to experience a greater sense of Christ consciousness as they become the tuning forks for others. Jesus exemplified Christ consciousness because he was in tune with this vibration. The healing that took place in his presence resulted from individual contact with these more refined energy patterns. In order to be a similar conduit for channeling these energies and for raising the frequency of one's own essence, it is necessary to remain clear and balanced in all respects—physically, emotionally, mentally, and spiritually.

The Origin of Earth Vortexes

The history of Earth's vortexes began at the moment the thought of such a planet was originated. That set off all the necessary forces to separate, project, direct, and intersect the Light properties desired for the planetary pattern. Since it was agreed that all aspects of previous creation would be incorporated into this pattern, each of the twelve Universes (the Universes of the Universes) supplied a ray of Light that contained all elements of its being. When all radiations of these Universes were seeded (focused) into the far reaches of the Milky Way galaxy, the energy forces, which eventually gave birth to the planet's physical manifestation, began to evolve.

Vortex Alterations for Free Will Experience

At this point in Earth's brief history, the vortexes were in perfect alignment with Universal Law. The flow of Light and Love was abundant and all of the planetary components were evolving naturally. Then, at a predetermined time, the primary vortexes were intentionally altered by the Creators so that Earth could be freed from strict adherence to its original blueprint. In the process, it was isolated from the rest of Creation and left to evolve without the assistance of the higher frequency energies that are normally available. The reasons for this action were twofold: (1) so that souls could experience "free will" completely independent of the influences of the One Mind (the collective consciousness of All That Is); and (2) so that others within the Universe would be less apt to interfere with the experiment. Thus the stage was set to experience the illusion of being separated consciously from the Source.

Since vortexes are the life-support systems of creation, they provide the basic energy units for the planet's survival. When they were realigned, they provided only minimum requirements for planetary evolution. In effect, they became dormant, waiting to receive the higher frequencies necessary to facilitate a subsequent planetary program.

Interference of the Lesser Gods

The changes to the vortexes also impacted certain entities outside of the immediate Earth realm. Although all who were not directly participating in this experiment were notified that they should remain outside the region of influence, a few souls did not heed the warnings. Following their own will, these souls entered the forbidden area and soon found themselves cut off from the higher energies which they were accustomed to. As a result, they slowly began to lose consciousness. The memory of who they were became distorted. The divine characteristic of Love was forgotten and the freedom associated with knowing the truth was lost.

In hopes of gaining back their freedom, the misplaced souls proceeded to mastermind control of Earth and her inhabitants. As an example, they were able to convince humans to look externally for a god who actually resides within. In this way the embodied souls became subservient to self-proclaimed gods who have been portrayed as wrathful, jealous, and judgmental. These lesser gods are so adept in projecting thought patterns into the planetary consciousness that most souls have remained in the darkness of ignorance during their entire sojourn on Earth—blindly obedient to religions and other institutions whose purpose is to control the masses.

Retreat to Inner Earth

When the primary vortexes were altered, the road maps between planets, star systems and Universes had to be redrawn. Thus it was not long before the Earth-based souls found themselves completely disoriented relative to the signposts—the stars. Some entities became so confused that they retreated to the inner Earth regions, where many remain today. They are joined by others who have moved "within" to seek refuge from thought forms of the lesser gods which were grossly afflicting the surface plane.

It is important to appreciate that all of what has taken place on Earth, regardless of how it is judged, has provided important elements to this most ambitious experiment. All activities, whether originally planned or the outbreak of circumstance, have fulfilled a purpose. As we regain the understanding of Self and our role within the greater plan, we will be able to accept this truth.

1989 Harmonization

Recently the primary vortexes were brought back into harmony with the natural order of the Universe. This was orchestrated by the Creators in cooperation with their Earth-based representatives. As of mid-year 1989 all sites were reactivated as a critical mass of Earth energy/consciousness attuned to the higher frequency Light projections. Thus a harmonizing rhythm has been imposed, and more orderliness has entered the system.

A vast human network is now firmly in place (aided by other kingdoms including the elemental and angelic) that is in harmony with the higher frequency projections. Those within this network are at one with the Christ vibration and thereby are beginning to receive the fourth-dimensional experience in this plane of existence. *The Christ has returned as a collective Messiah of human consciousness!*

With this phase of the planetary program complete, Earth with all of its life forms has taken a major step toward an expanded state of consciousness. Soon it will be able to overcome the density/limitations associated with our present existence, anchored in thoughts and actions emanating from fear, doubt, judgment, jealousy, the desire to control the free will of others, and so on. These old patterns will become more evident as they interact with other nonharmonious energies which have been dispelled recently from the higher realms (i.e., the lesser gods). All that is nonharmonious will remain in the third dimension until it is in harmony with the higher frequencies or is translated when Earth ascends. This most likely will create more chaos and confusion in those who are not adapting to the changes.

New Alignment with the Stargates

As part of the activation process the vortexes were fine-tuned to accommodate the changes which occurred throughout all of creation over the course of this planetary program. Earth is now in alignment with the key interdimensional doorways corresponding to Universal time/space/event sequences (including activities within parallel time zones). These doorways are also known as portals or stargates. They provide safe, orderly passage throughout the many and one Universe.

Portals Opened: First, Second and Third Calls

The portals on the surface plane and in the inner Earth region, as well as the astral realms, are now positioned to allow unrestricted movement of souls. This represents a major provision for the "first call" to souls who have evolved beyond the third-dimension Earth experience. The doorways are accessible to those who have made their departure preparations, as evidenced by their evolvement beyond third-dimensional patterns and their willingness to take responsibility for entering into the next octave of existence. Key to this preparation is the desire to let go of the human drama while embracing unlimited thinking.

A "second call" shall be made prior to the release of the last major energy forces necessary to complete the planetary balancing and cleansing. This next summons will support those souls who do not desire to experience that which shall ensue. The "third and final call" shall come forth prior to the transformation of third-dimension Earth, and will respond to entities whose options will be limited severely by the conditions prevalent in the final days. For those who do not resonate with these signals sent forth by the One Mind, there are provisions for the relocation of souls (with or without physical vessels) to other planetary realms of similar circumstance where the evolutionary process can be carried out according to the individual's will.

Effects of the Changes

These calls, in response to the changes that are taking place on Earth and beyond, should be taken quite seriously. The higher frequency energies are affecting all of Earth's creation, including embodied souls, without exception. Here are some reasons why:

(1) The Light is shining ever so brightly on the truth of one's presence in the Universal order. Once a person accepts that he or she is an integral part of a greater plan, then it will be clear why it is so important to be in harmony with what is taking place. The old patterns must be released (now) to make way for the changes. If this happens, the collective consciousness of the planet can expand and all will be positioned to move on to experience other realms. If there is resistance to the change, then it will be only through great ordeal that the purposes of the higher frequencies will be realized.

(2) The vortexes are providing greater life support for the planet as pure energies pour forth from the Source. When Earth fully embraces these higher energies, she can breathe new life into all her aspects, thereby releasing the limitations or densities previously accepted. All shall be made new!

(3) The vortexes can now transport beings of higher frequencies to Earth without the previous restrictions. This is most significant, as there are many who have come to this far region of the Universe to assist in the personal and planetary ascension process. But because these galactic emissaries have difficulty withstanding dense thought forms, Earthlings are being asked to prepare for their arrival by releasing all nonharmonious thought forms. Projecting Light and Love into everything and everyone is an absolute requirement.

Wisdom from the Experiment

In closing it is worth remembering that we have all participated on Earth's third-dimensional platform to gain an understanding of what it would be like to be separated consciously from the One Mind/Source/God/I Am That I AM—or whatever you use to describe the All That Is. We have survived our self-imposed experience, and in the process have explored the many facets of independent will. It is now time to take the wisdom which we have acquired and move back into harmony with the truth of All That Is. We are beings of Light and citizens of the Universe, and the way home is through the vortexes of our consciousness.

17

The Principles of Vortical Structure and Motion

Germane Through Lyssa Royal

Greetings to all of you. We have a model here of a vortex, so that we may refer to it. We provide a diagram [below] so that the reader will know to what we are referring.

We are first going to talk about the vortex idea in a broad way so that you will understand the dynamic of vortical energy and its application in reality. Then we will narrow the focus to Sedona and how the vortexes interact with you as individuals.

The Triad: Primal 3-D Template

Many of you have heard this over and over again: A primal template of your reality structure is the triad—one polarity, the other polarity, and the integrative point. The vortex model [see Fig. 1] is an offshoot of that idea. You can imagine the vortex as being a triangle. It is narrow at the top and wide at the base.

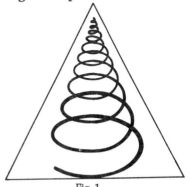

Fig. 1

Basically speaking, what you call the primary forces of physical existence stem from the vortical structure. Now, understand the idea you call solar system. You are all aware of looking at a solar-system structure like this—you look through the vortex and see concentric circles [Fig. 2].

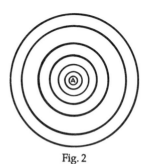

Fig. 2

This central point here [the tip of the vortex, labeled **A**] is the star, or sun. This is the way you view solar systems. However, the structure of solar systems is like a vortex, *not* concentric circles [see Fig. 3]. Therefore the energy of a solar system uses the same principles as the vortex, which has something to do with gravitational fields.

The Vortical Formula for Finding Habitable Planets

If you were a space traveler and came into a solar system, by using a mathematical formula of the vortical principle you could theorize what each planet's gravitational field and planetary conditions were. You would go into the solar system and see different planets in different orbits around the seed mass or sun. You would ask yourself, "Which

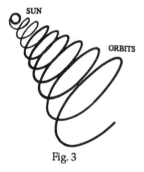

SUN

ORBITS

Fig. 3

one has a gravitational field that I as a human could exist on?" If you were to develop a mathematical formula that represents the idea of vortical energy, you would need to take into account first and foremost *where* the planetary orbit is along the vortex. You would also need to take into account the materials the planet is made of. Is it gaseous? Is it more solid matter? Then you would need to take into account its size. Those are the three primary ideas.

You will find, as a generalization, that the area closest to the star (the first one or two planets) would not be habitable. They would either be too gaseous or possess a very high density and high gravitational field. You will find that the third and fourth planets would be the most habitable planets on average, because the forming of solar systems is such that those are the ones that have the optimum conditions—the correct balance between size, mass/material, and their position in the vortical structure. When you balance the three variables, you would be able to tell from its orbit which planet has a gravitational field that could support your landing.

Gravity Determined by Planet's Vortical Position

This discusses principles that your science has not necessarily taken into account. Scientists do not *really* know what gravity is or what really causes it. In the past it has been thought that the centrifugal force of the orbit of your world is what creates gravity. Though that may assist in holding the planet *on* its orbital path, it is *not* necessary for the gravitational field of your planet. The gravitational field of a planet is related to its *position* in the vortical structure of the solar system and to the other two of the three main points we were talking about before (size and mass/material). Therefore you can see that your solar system is, in fact, a unit and not a bunch of independent planets circling a sun. In fact, the very *structure* of the solar system is dependent on all of its other parts.

If you see these different orbital areas (the circular parts of the vortex), the part where the vortex comes together (at the end of the cone) in your solar system can be considered the sun. Many of you know that the sun is comprised of gases. However, there are dimensional flips and phase shifts occurring in the area of the sun that allow the structure of the entire vortex to remain intact. Thus if there is solar activity, there can be shifting. You can see that the more dramatic the solar activity is, the more dramatic the shifting would be. Some of the natural catastrophes within solar systems have occurred because the solar energy shifted. This is only one idea. But you can see that solar activity can affect the entire structure of the solar system. Of course, you can apply that to the planetary systems: any planet that shifts its orbit, shifts the entire vortical structure.

The Apex: Point of Dimensional Change

That is one idea about using this model of the vortex. The point at the end or apex of the cone is an area of dimensional change. Optimally speaking, when you move through the point at the end of the cone, another cone emerges on the other side [see Fig. 4].

Fig. 4

The Mirror Vortex: A Parallel Universe

You have called these parallel universes, etc. These are stable structures. They primarily exist in duplicate like the above figure—one on each end with the points together. In your symbology this is often represented by the infinity symbol, which is a primary structure. Springing from those cones may be other ideas as well, but we won't get into that now. ∞

You can see now in macrocosmic terms how vital the vortex energy is to the stabilization of physical reality. Let us look now at the microcosmic level—the atomic structure.

The Vortex of the Atom

You have an atomic nucleus and electrons that fly around the nucleus [Fig. 5]. For the sake of the example, we will use this vortical model again [Fig. 6]. Look through the cone and you will notice that this is how atomic structure is presented in some textbooks—as concentric circles drawn by the electrons spinning in orbit. You have seen it in other configurations as well, but we are using this for our example. The point here at the end

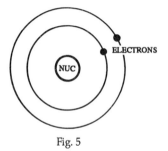

Fig. 5

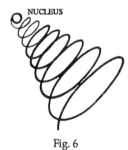

Fig. 6

of the cone (the nucleus of the atom) can be equated with the sun. They are *exactly* the same idea. It is just that you are dealing in different scales. Hence you can predict atomic movement and atomic change by understanding the principles that were earlier outlined for the solar system (size, mass/material properties, and position).

The Polar Vortexes

You have been given an example of the macrocosmic and microcosmic vortical structures. How does this interact with your world? Generally, there is a primary vortex in each hemisphere of your planet. If you have a globe separated into northern and southern hemispheres, you will find that the apex of each polar vortex is pointed toward the equator [deep inside the Earth]. Therefore, in the *middle* of the Earth you have another gateway, or doorway. That can be considered the seed mass or the vortical point from which many of the radiations of energy stream outward. You will find that at the poles of your planet there will be less of a concentration of energy. We are not necessarily talking about the surface of your planet, for the points of the vortex are deep within the planet, not touching the surface. However, the outer perimeter of the cone (the wide part) is represented at the poles. You will find that vortexes are made up of other vortexes. It is always this macrocosmic/microcosmic principle.

Macro Vortexes Activate Micro Vortexes

Sasha has talked a little bit about why some of the vortexes appear in certain areas in your planet with the various intersections of lines, etc. Let us talk about how you are activated on a microcosmic level by the macrocosm when *you* walk into a vortex area. That is what really occurs. There is a recognition of energy that resonates within the smaller model within you of the *same* framework.

Let us give you an example. Let us say that you walk into the Airport Mesa vortex. (Again, it will depend on the different principles of each of the vortexes.) That particular vortex is an electrical, or "masculine" vortex. We will also use the labels "expansive" and "contractive" for vortexes. Airport Mesa would be considered an expansive vortex, not a contractive one. Contractive tends to go within and is more the feminine principle; expansive tends to be a going without and is more the masculine principle.

How You Are Affected by Specific Vortexes

When you go into the airport vortex area, the inherent energy of that area (expansive) will dictate first the *type* of experience you have the *potential* to have. When you walk into that vortex all the minor vortexes in your body are activated. It is as if all of them are simultaneously tapped on the shoulder and given the message, "Wake up!" They all stand at attention. After the initial acclimation period, some of those that are not directly aligned to that expansive vortex will go about their business and leave the body vortexes that are more aligned with that energy to be the sole operators in this experience.

You are aware of the vortical points in the body called the chakras. They basically conform to the same idea of the cone and seed mass. These are the main energy-vortex areas of the body. You will also find that each and every atom in your body is a "minivortex"; so in that sense you are made up entirely of vortical energy. Thus when you insert yourself within a natural environmental vortex, a resonance field is created that allows your bodies to begin to vibrate in a much more natural state than they are used to, as it is their natural environment. A *nonvortical* energy can be considered (from this viewpoint) an "unnatural" environment.

To give you an analogy, let us say you have your arms full of packages while you are walking down the street. Suddenly you come face to face with an idea, a vision (whatever you wish to call it) that is absolutely the most perfect thing that could *ever* occur in your life at that moment and it emotionally stirs you. Continuing with our analogy, that shock causes you to drop the packages and to absorb the energy.

This is what occurs when you walk into a vortex energy. The entire structure of your bodies drops the "packages" and simply becomes momentarily blissful in its state of absorption.

When you get your wits about you, you begin picking up the packages. But the portions of you that are most aligned with that particular energy stay focused in it. This is an analogy that may allow you to understand what we have talked about.

Does a vortex imply a spiraling energy? If so, does it spiral both upward and downward?

The vortical energy will allow itself to spiral in a cycle where, could you put a direction on it, one side contracts and the other expands. In terms of time and space, the two eventually meet. However, the natural structure in its "complete state" (if you could consider it complete) would be two vortexes point to point.

So you mean that it goes in and out dimensionally?

Yes. Sometimes it will occur in the same dimension, but most of the time it won't.

Would your model there be more accurately portrayed as a spiral rather than concentric circles?

Yes. However, if you look at a slinky (which spirals) through the hole in the middle, it would appear to some degree concentric.

Is there a counterrotating vortex within a vortex?

Clockwise and Counterclockwise

We won't go into that too far, but we will say that is an applicable theoretical idea. Basically speaking, you will find that one vortex revolves (if you wish to use that term) in one direction and the other vortex at the other end rotates in the opposite direction. This is demonstrated in your Earth plane in terms of northern and southern hemispheres—the energy there exists as opposites.

Would Giza be like that? Doesn't it have a pyramid underneath it?

More of an etheric pyramid. It is a different template, but the same idea applies somewhat.

Would it be like an etheric/energetic reflection or a duplicate?

Yes. Although the type of vortex we have been discussing is point to point, that pyramid is base to base.

Vortical energy has an output, right? The energy is coming from somewhere and is going somewhere?

In a *linear* sense.

So how does that occur?

We sense that you are asking your question from a third-dimensional perspective, which has no relevance in the actual reality of the vortex itself. It does not necessarily need a cause and effect.

In that case, explain to me how it works from our point of view.

Contraction-Expansion, a Pulsing Movement

You know the idea of contraction/expansion? That is the movement inherent in a vortical structure. That does not need a reason. It simply *is*.

So it is like a spiraling outward and then a spiraling inward.

Yes. A breathing in, out, in, out. A pulse.

But the energy would be most focused at the peak of the cone. It would be most intense there.

Dimensional Doorways at Focal Points

Yes. That is why at those peaks, or those tips of the cones, the dimensional doorways occur.

So we could access the energy at its focal point more than at its base?

Yes. At its base you would find it somewhat dissipated and you would really, in a sense, have no use for it. There is always a use for energy, but you will find that you would probably prefer to work more with the condensing aspect of the vortex.

Is this the same principle as white and black holes?

The Sun: A Black Hole-White Hole Focal Point

Yes. Since the sun or the seed mass is the tip of the vortex, it is the transitional point—the black hole/white hole. That is another idea that is mirrored macrocosmically/microcosmically.

So the pyramid shape facilitates a vortex to start spiraling? Does the shape of the pyramid itself induce the energy to start spiraling upward, to focus at its peak?

The Pyramid: A Third-Dimensional Vortex

You can use pyramid energy for your own purposes in the third-dimensional reality more easily than you can use vortex energy, because the condensation point is within your reality (on the Earth surface) rather than in other dimensions or underground. You see, you are exposed on the Earth plane to vortical energy from the base, or the wide part of the cone. The condensed part (the tip or apex) is either within the Earth or within alternate dimensions. Pyramid energy can allow you to focus energy from the tip of the pyramid *in* your physical reality so that you may use it.

If you took that model and put one end of it into the Earth so that the central sun was in the center of the Earth, then you've got another one coming out the other side of the Earth?

Yes.

Then what we are dealing with is that wide, dissipated part here on the surface of the Earth?

The Seed Mass at Earth's Center

Yes. To use the model, the tip of the cone is the center of the Earth. This is similar to the idea of the center of your brain, a gateway. The entire area of the widest part of the cone represents the planet itself. Thus the planet is exposed to the same amount of vortical energy from the seed mass *within* the planet.

So why do we have some vortexes more powerful than others?

Those are *surface* vortexes that are outcroppings, or (to get somewhat esoteric) probabilities of the matrical vortex, if you will. Sasha explained somewhat how they are created. The only thing we will say at this time is that the connection between the main planetary vortex we have just described and the minor vortexes is the same as the connection between your own major vortex as a being and your chakras as minor vortexes. Your atomic structure is a further system of minor vortexes—it is the macrocosmic/microcosmic idea.

Would it work as an analogy to place the point of the cone in the heart?

Yes. It can work.

Earth Vortexes Focus at Core

In the energy matrix of the planet, how many major vortexes are there? I am curious about the primary ones that have their focal point at the core of the planet.

All of them have their focal point at the center of the planet. However, in terms of how many you could *physically* go to, we would say that there are twelve major ones. There are other vortexes that do not correspond with your *physical* planet. Those are considered *dimensional* vortexes.

Looking at your example of penetrating the Earth and considering that there are twelve of them, I am reminded of a paper written by a geologist. He describes particular places on the surface of the planet where there is one end of a vortex on one side, and directly opposite on the other side of the planet is the other vortex. Do you agree with that idea?

Not necessarily. Some of the vortexes will line up that way, some will not. This is because some of their energies will dissipate before they reach the planetary surface.

But these have an outlet someplace?

Yes. Whether it is inside your planet or dimensionally somewhere else.

What is the effect of the vortexes that lie opposite to each other on the planet?

An individual coming into an area that has an opposite area somewhere else may experience memories from the other vortex. There is an exchange of energy, a movement of energy, a fluid gate that *may* exist.

Would that explain the oceanlike memories or feelings that people have here?

Yes. It is one idea.

What is the relationship of the vortex energy and the crystal shape?

Vortex Activates Crystal Structure, Then DNA

The crystal shape has more to do with the DNA structure. If you study it more closely you will find that the crystal structure can be the vehicle toward the activation of the DNA structure. The vortical energy will be the instigator of the crystal structure's activation.

If that is the model—that point is the central sun within the planet, and the outer circles are the planets—do they connect with the solar sun? Is there a further extension of that same shape, or has it been inverted again?

We are not necessarily saying they are all *physically* connected, as is reflected in the model. But you will find that they exist *within* each other as microcosmic ideas. For instance, we have outlined the idea of the hypothetical center representing the meeting of the two vortexes—the idea of the center of the Earth, the center of the brain, the center of your solar system, the center of your galaxy (the galactic core) *and* the center of an atom.

Are these vortex points on Earth her chakras?

Structural Similarity of 3rd- and 4th-Density Planets

In a sense, yes. You will find that every planet has different vortical structures. Basically, planets that exist within third and fourth density within a certain range of dimensions will manifest this basic vortical structure.

You know how you make different shapes of pasta by squeezing it through the machine? We are saying that the consciousnesses here over millennia formed an etheric crystallized shape dimensionally. When an energy comes through that shape, it spins with a certain shape, color and frequency. That is why vortexes are different. Is that analogy clear?

Yes. The following is rather a crude analogy, but if you had a membrane like an onion skin wrapped around your Earth and astronauts came, they would have to break a hole in the membrane. Even if the membrane healed over, there would still be a "scar" that would guide the movement of the energy of a planet.

I have a question about the ability of geometric forms to induce the spiraling vortex energy. I am guessing that all arched, vaulted, domed, conical and pyramidal shapes induce a certain vortex energy. Can we see the difference being a frequency? A vibration? How would the different forms affect the spiraling energy?

Influence of Geometric Form vs. Initial Template/Seed Mass

The differences would have to do with the initial template or the initial seed mass—its form, its shape and its initial energy emissions. They will not be all the same; they do not have the same properties.

It depends on the energy of the geometric shape. If its condensation or momentum of energy is more powerful than the vortical structure, the latter will mold itself around the geometric shape. If the momentum of the vortical structure, on the other hand, has more energy than the geometric pattern or template, the latter will shift itself to adapt to the vortical structure.

Is the conical shape the more primary of the vortical structures?

Yes.

So the others are more or less derivative of the conical shape?

Somewhat derivative, yes. They are translations of this more basic idea into a third-density reality.

Even though the four-sided pyramid was apparently chosen as a suitable vehicle to transform energy?

Fourth Density Will Bring the Three-Sided Pyramid

Yes, but you will find that as you move into fourth density, the four-sided pyramid will be used less and the three-sided pyramid will be used more.

So could we consider the three-sided pyramid to increase the frequency or the rate of spin?

The three-sided pyramid basically represents the more primal template of reality, which will transform itself into the cone from the three-sided pyramid as you transform.

Is there anything you can give us that we can begin to apply alchemically to manifest in our physical environment?

There are alchemical equations you can use that utilize the vortical structures. However, you are approaching what can be considered magic in its more shaded sense, which we would not encourage.

Energy and power area halfway into Boynton Canyon

Vortex at the
"Saddle" in
Boynton Canyon

Cathedral Rock with
Red Rock Crossing in
the foreground

Cathedral Rock with Courthouse Butte in the background

Cathedral Rock from the north

Bell Rock from Village of Oak Creek

Bell Rock from
halfway to the top

Airport Vortex

Schnebly Hill from south Sedona

Schnebly Hill Merry-
go-round

Schnebly Hill Valley

Courthouse Butte as seen from the Chapel area

Courthouse Butte from Bell Rock

"The Sentinal" at Chapel of the Holy Cross area

Jnnamed rock forma-
ion near Red Canyon

The Cockscomb from Red Canyon

Upper Wilson Canyon from Steamboat Rock

Wilson Mountain
from Sedona

Indian petroglyph at
Honaki in Loy
Canyon — possibly
turtle deity

Indian petroglyphs in Loy Canyon

Jacks Canyon Spires

Sedona and Capitol Butte from Bear Mountain

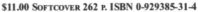

THE EXPLORER RACE SERIES

ZOOSH AND HIS FRIENDS THROUGH ROBERT SHAPIRO

THE SERIES: Humans—creators-in-training—have a purpose and destiny so heartwarmingly, profoundly glorious that it is almost unbelievable from our present dimensional perspective. Humans are great lightbeings from beyond this creation, gaining experience in dense physicality. This truth about the great human genetic experiment of the Explorer Race and the mechanics of creation is being revealed for the first time by Zoosh and his friends through superchannel Robert Shapiro. These books read like adventure stories as we follow the clues from this creation that we live in out to the Council of Creators and beyond.

❶ THE EXPLORER RACE

You individuals reading this are truly a result of the genetic experiment on Earth. You are beings who uphold the principles of the Explorer Race. The information in this book is designed to show you who you are and give you an evolutionary understanding of your past that will help you now. The key to empowerment in these days is to not know everything about your past, but to know what will help you now. Your number-one function right now is your status of Creator apprentice, which you have achieved through years and lifetimes of sweat. You are constantly being given responsibilities by the Creator that would normally be things that Creator would do. The responsibility and the destiny of the Explorer Race is not only to explore, but to create. 574 P. $25.00 ISBN 0-929385-38-1

❷ ETs and the EXPLORER RACE

In this book, Robert channels Joopah, a Zeta Reticulan now in the ninth dimension who continues the story of the great experiment—the Explorer Race—from the perspective of his civilization. The Zetas would have been humanity's future selves had not humanity re-created the past and changed the future. 237 P. $14.95 ISBN 0-929385-79-9

❸ EXPLORER RACE: ORIGINS and the NEXT 50 YEARS

This volume has so much information about who we are and where we came from—the source of male and female beings, the war of the sexes, the beginning of the linear mind, feelings, the origin of souls—it is a treasure trove. In addition, there is a section that relates to our near future—how the rise of global corporations and politics affects our future, how to use benevolent magic as a force of creation and how we will go out to the stars and affect other civilizations. Astounding information. 339 P. $14.95 ISBN 0-929385-95-0

❹ EXPLORER RACE: CREATORS and FRIENDS
The MECHANICS of CREATION

Now that you have a greater understanding of who you are in the larger sense, it is necessary to remind you of where you came from, the true magnificence of your being. You must understand that you are creators-in-training, and yet you were once a portion of Creator. One could certainly say, without being magnanimous, that you are still a portion of Creator, yet you are training for the individual responsibility of being a creator, to give your Creator a coffee break. This book will allow you to understand the vaster qualities and help you remember the nature of the desires that drive any creator, the responsibilities to which a creator must answer, the reaction a creator must have to consequences and the ultimate reward of any creator. 435 P. $19.95 ISBN 1-891824-01-5

❺ EXPLORER RACE: PARTICLE PERSONALITIES

All around you in every moment you are surrounded by the most magical and mystical beings. They are too small for you to see as single individuals, but in groups you know them as the physical matter of your daily life. Particles who might be considered either atoms or portions of atoms consciously view the vast spectrum of reality yet also have a sense of personal memory like your own linear memory. These particles remember where they have been and what they have done in their infinitely long lives. Some of the particles we hear from are Gold, Mountain Lion, Liquid Light, Uranium, the Great Pyramid's Capstone, This Orb's Boundary, Ice and Ninth-Dimensional Fire. 237 P. $14.95 ISBN 0-929385-97-7

❻ EXPLORER RACE and BEYOND

With a better idea of how creation works, we go back to the Creator's advisers and receive deeper and more profound explanations of the roots of the Explorer Race. The liquid Domain and the Double Diamond portal share lessons given to the roots on their way to meet the Creator of this universe, and finally the roots speak of their origins and their incomprehensibly long journey here. 360 P. $14.95 ISBN 1-891824-06-6

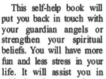

Publishing Presents

Plus Hundreds More!

A New Formula For Creation
Judith Moore

This book brings an inspiring positive message regarding the future of our planet. Earth is experiencing the Shift of the Ages, a time marked by massive Earth changes and social upheaval. This is foretold in many prophecies, including Hopi prophecies and the biblical Revelations. They warn that raising consciousness is the only way to avert a massive cataclysm.

$16.95 Softcover, 186 p. ISBN: 1-891824-57-0

Living in the Heart
(With CD)
Drunvalo Melchizedek

This is a book of remembering. You have always had this place within your heart, and it is still there now. It existed before creation, and it will exist even after the last star shines its brilliant light. This book is written with the least amount of words possible to convey the meaning and to keep the integrity of the essence of this experience. The images are purposefully simple. It is written from the heart, not the mind.

$25.00 Softcover, 120 p. ISBN: 1-891824-43-0

Ancient Secret of the Flower of Life *Vol. I*
Drunvalo Melchizedek

Once, all life in the universe knew the Flower of Life as the creation pattern —the geometrical design leading us into and out of physical existence. Sacred Geometry is the form beneath our being and points to a divine order in our reality. We can follow that order from the invisible atom to the infinite stars, finding ourselves at each step.

$25.00 Softcover, 228 p. ISBN: 1-891824-17-1

Change Your Encodements, Your DNA, Your Life!
Amma through
Cathy Chapman

The first part of this book discusses what you call love. Love is the most powerful energy. The second part contains powerful techniques for working with your DNA encodements. The third part contains what some call predictions, which are nothing more than my reading and interpretation of the energy at the time when the energy was read.

$16.95 Softcover, 303 p. ISBN: 1-891824-52-X

Animal Souls Speak
Explorer Race Series
Robert Shapiro

Welcome to the footsteps of the loving beings (animals) who support you, who wish to reveal more about themselves to you and who welcome you, not only to planet Earth, but more specifically to the pathway of self-discovery. The animal world will speak through elders, since that way they can include knowledge and wisdom about their home planets. Each animal brings a wonderous gift to share with humanity—enjoy it!

$29.95 Softcover, 610 p. ISBN: 1-891824-50-3

Ancient Secret of the Flower of Life *Vol. II*
Drunvalo Melchizedek

Drunvalo shares the instructions for the Mer-Ka-Ba meditation, step-by-step techniques for the re-creation of the energy field of the evolved human. From the pyramids and mysteries of Egypt to the new race of Indigo children, Drunvalo presents the sacred geometries of the Reality and the subtle energies that shape our world.

$25.00 Softcover, 477 p. ISBN: 1-891824-21-X

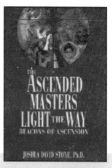